the ONE

the ONE

FINDING SOUL MATE LOVE
AND MAKING IT LAST

Kathy Freston

miramax books

HYPERION

NEW YORK

For Star Angel T.

Contents

the ONE

chapter one

What It's All About

When love beckons to you, follow him, / Though his ways are hard and steep. / And when his wings enfold you yield to him, / Though the sword hidden among his pinions may wound you. / And when he speaks to you believe in him, / Though his voice may shatter your dreams as the north wind lays waste the garden. . . . All these things shall love do unto you that you may know the secrets of your heart, and in that knowledge become a fragment of Life's heart.

KAHLIL GIBRAN, *THE PROPHET*

The One. The love of our life, the fulfillment of our dreams. That glorious person who will set our soul on fire and stoke our passion for life. We get up in the morning to the song of this promise on the radio and lull ourselves to sleep at night with novels and films about two disenchanted people who finally find each other and, in the process, make the world a better place. We hope against hope that one day this will be our story. We long for this connection we've heard about, with all its magic and mystery and mojo; we want to be lit up and transformed simply by

1

being in the presence of that heaven-sent "one and only." Ah, soul mate love.

The longing to taste this sort of bliss, to partake in this sort of partnership, is deeply ingrained. It is as if our psyches are coded with the desire to overcome our sense of separateness from each other. Finding a partner and thriving together seems to be our central mission, a natural instinct that powers our daily lives and drives us forward. We find ourselves going to nearly any length to have this crazy, wonderful thing called love.

If you have ever had a maddening crush or experienced the marvel of sexual union, you know that the energy is not of this world. It is a miracle that presents itself to you, leaving you feeling blessed and chosen. While falling in love, we sense we are being drawn into something bigger than ourselves, as if we are being called upon to participate in something important unfolding within and all around us. We can feel ourselves changing as the relationship plunges us headlong into situations that trigger bold realizations and glimpses of enlightenment. When love is in the air, we find ourselves at the center of the universe with all the wheels of creation in full motion.

Suddenly we remember we are meant to lift ourselves up from our denser vibration and become lighter. We are meant to shatter any barriers that keep us from being happy and peaceful. We are meant to become ever more conscious and in turn spark consciousness in those around us. We are meant to touch each other deeply and inspire the next generation of creators and healers. And in this way romantic love—and the search for it—plays its part by *stirring us to wakefulness*.

Any time you are rocked by romantic love, you are being urged by Providence to open your eyes so that you can expand as a person. When you are silly with infatuation or furious over a missed connection with your lover, you can be sure that this is just part of the curriculum of enlightenment. Such is the call of Spirit to go beyond the limits of our individual egos and unpack some particular aspect of our evolution.

Love can play itself out in so many scenarios (warm and excited conversations, great sex, screaming fights, tumultuous breakups, to name just a few), that it's not always easy to see its underlying message. I believe it is this: You are not successful in love just because you find a partner and stick with them for a lifetime; you are successful in love when it provides you with a way to keep learning about yourself and the world around you, becoming more connected with the Oneness of all of life, so that each experience you have—glorious, sad, or frustrating—becomes a strand in the web of your evolution. How you navigate the ins and outs of love is what gives purpose to your time on earth.

It doesn't matter whether or not you are in a committed relationship at the moment of reading this book. You may be married or you may be looking for a partner; you may be wondering if you are in the right relationship or you may be trying to make the one you're in more magical. But know this one thing for sure: any and all roads will lead to your spiritual awakening. All that is required is a desire to experience deep and profound love.

What matters most is that which is getting stirred up within you. Each time your buttons are pushed or your lust is ignited, you can be sure your soul is rumbling to give birth to some new level of awareness. The soul mate does you the unwitting service of poking and prodding until you open up. They bring you to your edge—your sense of limitation—and then push you to go farther. Sometimes it's gentle, kind, and generous; but sometimes it's just plain maddening.

Every single interaction, every exchange between you and that significant other has meaning and purpose. The mirror of relationships shows us where we need to grow, and guides us forward. The soul mate relationship—whether it manifests as joyful or heart-rending—is a *portal through which we access our spiritual potential*.

I believe that the romantic quest is a gateway into heaven, through which we can tap into our true Self. When I say Self with a capital S, I mean the divine within us—who we really are beyond the personality and learned traits that shape our public persona. The Self is our *primordial truth*; it is our center, our innocence, and our perfection. It is that which is divine in each and every one of us.

This subtle essence of divinity is the infinite and immortal seed of love which Hindu sages call *Atman*, Christian mystics refer to as *Christ Consciousness*, Buddhist scholars hold as *Buddha Nature*, and Judaic tradition calls *ruach*. This identification with God is our highest potential; it is our actuality that we must ultimately embrace even as we travel through the story of our humanity. It is said that we are all made in God's image, and thus within us is the individualized presence of Spirit, or God. I sometimes refer to God as Spirit because the word *Spirit* seems less a personification and more the all pervading *All-That-Is*. This, our divine heritage, whispers to us to recall that at the inmost part of ourselves we are fundamentally *One* with God and with everything. Such is the unity consciousness that draws us to one another.

The concept of soul mates has its origins in Greek mythology, according to which human beings were originally born with two heads, four arms, and four legs. When these humans offended the gods, they were split down the middle and condemned to spend eternity searching for their other halves in order to become whole again. Such myths resonate with our own feeling that we have been split off from something essential; perhaps it is the awareness of the divinity within us. Because some of us have lost track of who we are at our core, we feel incomplete, disconnected. And so it is that the quest for soul mate love feels like a religious experience, and in a very real way, it is: *we find our way back to our Oneness with God by learning to connect and discover our union with each other.*

Should you choose to be alert to this curriculum, you will come to understand where you need to grow in order to fulfill your spiritual goal. You can then break through the patterns that have held you back from Self-realization (the full integration of one's humanity with one's divinity). By seeing your mistakes in the mirror of partnership you will learn to correct them. You will become a more loving person by learning to overcome your tendency to judge, control, or cause pain. You will learn to interpret the world using the language of love and thus replace any antipathy with kindness. And even if you *don't* choose to take an active role in this process, you will still get the lessons you need; you'll just keep getting them over and over again until you take them to heart.

The quest for a soul mate is a narrative we follow that helps us dissolve the boundaries between our individual selves and God. If we can learn to love even one person wholeheartedly and without condition, we will have succeeded in allowing Spirit to be known in and through us. Partnership with a person is a metaphor, or microcosm, for partnership with God. Romantic love is one of many

spiritual schools; in it we can learn to embrace, substan-
tiate, and reinvigorate our divine heritage.

As a counselor of personal growth and spirituality, I
work with clients using body, mind, and spirit to affect
change in their lives. Having seen so many people struggling with their relationships, I've come to realize that the
desperation they feel when things aren't going well is in
fact an excellent catalyst for delving deeply into their
problems in a productive way. It certainly worked that
way for me many years ago, when it dawned on me that
if I didn't start doing things differently, there was a very
real possibility that things could get dangerously worse
than they already were. I was in an abusive relationship,
running out of money, and in fragile health. I had lost
most of my friends and nearly all my self-respect.

Then, by the grace of God, I began running into various spiritual teachers and really worked at taking in their
messages for healing. I, in turn, undertook my own program to turn things around. I prayed and meditated. I attended workshops and classes and intensive retreats. I
read every self-help book in sight and taped inspirational
messages all over my home and car.

And things began to change. Sometimes the shifts were
barely perceptible; at other times I was bowled over by
the miracles showing up in my life. I was finally able to
leave my abusive boyfriend; I started making money do-

ing meaningful work; and my health rebounded. When people commented on the changes in me, I realized that I had intuitively found my way into a process that was highly effective in creating transformation. So I wrote and produced a series of guided meditation CDs and began volunteering my services to any and all who needed them. After a while I went into business helping clients make changes in their lives, and wrote *Expect a Miracle: 7 Spiritual Steps for Finding the Right Relationship.*

I began to notice a pervasive wistfulness when people talked about relationships: they seemed to pin their hopes on finding and keeping the ideal partner—what is commonly referred to as the One—and it got my wheels turning. Over and over, I would hear the details of struggle in finding the perfect partner. There was such a deep longing, almost a desperation about the search. I think that longing is what Tibetan Buddhists call the "hungry ghost"; it is the incessant, and sometimes manic, yearning we feel when we search for someone or something to make us feel whole and happy. No matter how hard we try to shape our partners (or potential partners) into an ideal form—or replace them in hopes of something better—the longing remains unsatisfied. And so it will be, until we realize that no other person on earth can fill the void we've created by forgetting the whole of who we are and what we are part of. We are—all of us—*extensions and manifestations of Spirit*. And until we step up to that holy birthright, we will keep on searching for a soul mate who seems ever beyond our reach.

It became obvious to me that this problem needed to be addressed—it's almost as if the ideas thrust themselves into my mind. I realized that somewhere along the way, we as a society had lost sight of the truth. Instead of finding peace within ourselves, we looked for happiness in the form of another person, situation, or thing. We would work hard to "get" someone, but then the relationship would "fail." Either the magic seemed to wear off or we never took the chance to commit to a partner because there might be a better deal just around the corner. Or, saddest of all, we suffered quietly in an unfulfilling marriage, dreaming of what might possibly set us free.

I receive many letters asking me agonizing questions about how to know if this or that partner is the right one, or whether or not sexual attraction is necessary for a happy marriage, or if compromising ideals could cost someone the love of their life. Most of all, I am asked if there really is someone for everyone. These are not idle musings; these questions haunt us at night when we can't sleep. They shadow us as we go about our daily lives and insist on being considered. The desire for profound love is painful when we haven't met anyone, and all-consuming once we have and are trying to maintain the fantasy of what love should be.

No matter what the question, this is the answer: *we*

are here in each other's lives to facilitate in one another a higher state of consciousness. We are here to open each other's eyes to God. We don't talk about that; it certainly isn't the spoken goal of most partnerships. But that *is* what is at play.

The spiritual task underlying romantic partnership is to close the psychic gap between one another and in so doing to close the gap between our humanity and our divinity. As we awaken the highest and most true part of ourselves and become more God-like, we evolve up through our grosser and more base tendencies into more developed ones. How better to achieve intimacy with our higher nature than to cultivate intimacy with the person who stands before us? You might have assumed that soul mate love was about finding the love of your life and setting up house together—and it is—but you will also come to see that part of the bargain is nothing less than spiritual salvation.

So this book is not about simply keeping the love you find (in fact, keeping a particular relationship might not end up being desirable at all), but about the process of truly experiencing the deep and abiding love we know exists but sometimes feel only in the beginning of the romance. I'm not here to demystify soul mates; I'm here instead to help you discover the very love you've heard about and make it grow and last. The One *is* indeed waiting for you, it's just a matter of your being able to recognize that person and step up to the plate. The One is that special person, but you are the One as well. By following the process laid out in this book, you will *become* the very love you want. You will draw to you the exact match that will speak into your soul's longing. And through it all, you will realize a greater Oneness—the inborn and ever expanding connection with Spirit, or God.

The challenge of finding and keeping a soul mate is the perfect impetus for our metaphysical maturation. Our love relationships bring us face to face with our demons, and we are willing to confront them and learn how to better ourselves because we want so badly to fulfill love's magical promise. It is by *using* the experiences that arise within the context of partnership—both the joyful and painful ones—that we come to embrace the enormous spiritual capacity that lies within us, making us capable of magnificent things, not only in the arena of relationships, but in every area of life.

The love relationships we give birth to in our dreams lead us to higher ground. They push us to find out who we are and what we are made of, to awaken to our power, *if* we choose to do so.

There is only one way to find soulful love, and that is through Spirit. Spirit is where we came from and within Spirit we will continue to journey. The "right relationship" is a bridge connecting us to our highest potential.

We are all chosen for love; the question is whether or not we show up to claim it.

May the following pages guide you along the way. May the light of truth illumine your path. And may you know with all your heart and soul the One who awaits you.

chapter two

The Divine Design

*"Everything that touches us, me and you, / takes us together
like a violin's bow, / which draws ONE voice out of two separate strings. / Upon what instrument are we two spanned? /
And what musician holds us in his hand?"*

—RAINER MARIA RILKE, *LOVE SONG*

Finding our soul mate promises to unlock
all the hidden treasures we always hoped were awaiting
us. It's as if by connecting to this person, we sense that we
will at long last find ourselves in a paradise indescribable
by all but a poet's language. Finally someone will free us
with their love, lifting us, exalted, to our very highest potential. We will come to know ourselves as generous and
selfless, as a far more evolved person than we've ever been
before. We might finally feel truly understood, deeply
known. Our loneliness will vanish, giving way to sublime
companionship, and we will forget all the unfulfilled

cravings of a lesser life. At last, we will feel complete and finally come to know the One. This is the archetypal partnership that powers our dreams; no matter what intellect tells us, we still believe that this kind of love exists.

And it does. Soul mate love may be the stuff of fairy tales, but the reason it is so consistently the stuff of myth and legend is because we *remember* that kind of love. We can sense, with every fiber of our being, the veracity of it.

When romantic love is fresh, it is like a sneak peek into heaven, a taste of an enlightened state of consciousness, a brief visit to love without boundaries. The ecstasy we experience at the beginning of a relationship is really the truth of what lies between any two souls. The sense of blinding connection and limitless potential is real. The problem, though, is that all too often we fall back into our old patterns of relating once the sense of ecstatic fusion of the first few months loses its grip on us. We stop working at being our best. And even though we know our habitual patterns may not be healthy or productive, it's all too easy to keep repeating them. When we act out of habit, we know who we are. And unless we are vigilant in the ways I will describe throughout this book, those learned limitations will keep us tethered to a predictable and unfulfilling love life. If we want more than just a glimpse of heaven, we must overcome our tendency to merely act on automatic pilot.

Our task, if we want to enter into a long-term relationship with the One, is to learn to stretch beyond our self-imposed limitations; we have to become competent in opening ourselves and *remaining* open to love, letting it move into and through us. For as we practice new ways of relating, we will become increasingly comfortable with a higher form of love. We will come to understand that the more we can relax into whatever is presenting itself to us, the more readily we will be able to sustain bliss. As the great Taoist philosopher Chuang Tzu said, "Do not struggle. Go with the flow of things, and you will find yourself at one with the mysterious unity of the Universe."

Soul Mates

In *The Tibetan Book of the Dead* the soul is described as being hungry for experiences it still needs in order to attain enlightenment. In collaboration with the wisdom of Spirit—it intuits what it needs to forward its advancement and attracts circumstances that assist it in moving to the next level of development. Our soul, which is the energetic body underlying our more superficial personality and physical body, journeys through many different iterations as it evolves into a more and more unfettered manifestation of love. In this journey, there are many things to learn; certainly, there are obstacles that must be overcome and issues that must be resolved before moving on. And these impediments will reveal themselves as major themes in our lives until we are able to work through and release them.

Some of us, for example, might experience one such impediment as the inability to forgive; if so, we will attract experiences that will give us ample opportunity to either hold a grudge or forgive. Others of us might tend to be selfish, or controlling. Such stances would "call" for the universe to keep providing us with opportunities which would tempt us to be tightfisted or bossy. We will either give in to those temptations and stay in our holding pattern, or we will make the shift and begin to respond to life in a more evolved manner. These choices will often show up within the context of a romantic relationship.

By holding our interest so intently, the soul mate is able to lead us right into the places where we need to grow. They not only testify to our brilliance and nurture our ability to love and be kind, but they also tweak us so that we can see where we are held back. In this way, the soul mate comes bearing the gift of our potential enlightenment. And in the most perfect way, as if by divine design, we each get what we need from the other. We support and inspire each other right alongside with pushing each other into the places that need our attention.

There is an essence, like a scent between animals that draws one soul to another. We have, at some level, agreed to play the mating game, seducing from each other all that we have yet to accomplish in terms of spiritual growth. It is as if a web of interconnecting impulses and choices was spun at the beginning of time, and there are certain people who have the right combination of ingredients—be they personality, unmet needs, or circumstances—to provide a ground from which each of the partners will gain growth and enlightenment. And so it is that we perform the dance of soul mates: we attract, seduce, grab hold, stir things up, and figure a way through it all. Each series of dance steps brings us closer to the truth and beauty of who we are.

In order to stay engaged with that soul who will help us on our mission of spiritual growth and development, there must be an irresistible attraction. Our heartstrings must be tugged with such intensity that our motivation to stay on the path—and in the relationship—remains stoked. We have to care so much about this person that we hang in there come hell or high water. Whatever the attraction is—sexual chemistry, deep friendship, financial stability, or shared lifestyle goals—it has to be alluring to the extent that two people will stay and deal with whatever comes up. Because things *will* come up. They are supposed to; the challenges are what keeps the growth alive.

Through knowing the soul mate, life's most profound work begins to unfold. We do indeed become a better version of ourselves by interacting with this person, and we are certainly moved to be kinder and more loving. But we also embark on our most sacred mission: working through all that remains incomplete or unenlightened within us. The soul mate brings up our issues, fortifies our drive to become more pure, and pushes us past what we thought were our limits. We need not go looking for that right person to fit the bill, for Spirit is always drawing us into the perfect match. Through the soulful relationship, we will become intimate with the One—the one standing in front of us, the one in the mirror, and most importantly, the Oneness of Spirit that connects all of us with each other.

Not all soul mate connections are obvious at first glance. Yes, some soul mates will find each other wildly captivating and sexy; but there are also people with whom we share an intellectual or emotional rapport that binds us together in a way that is different from but perhaps just as formidable as plain old lust. Soul mates come in all shapes and sizes and no one can judge their "rightness." What qualifies a relationship as soulful is how much our heart is opened by being with someone. All relationships serve as a portal to divinity, but romantic love is so ideal because it gets our attention in such an enthralling way. It winds us up, stimulates us, and delivers us primed for all sorts of revelations.

Relationships have so much to do with perspective; we see according to our own personal and subjective mindset. Have you ever known someone as a friend for a long time and then, for whatever reason, suddenly started to look at that person differently? Romantically? Perhaps they irritated you in some way when you first met them, so you relegated them to the "friend" category. You didn't like the way they dressed, perhaps, or you thought they were a bit silly or stand-offish. But then somehow someone you had considered not terribly important became wondrously enthralling. They didn't change; your perception did. Right before your very eyes, an ordinary relationship became extraordinary. That kind of shift is a powerful example of how love can be found right in front of you if you can just suspend your typical judgments and rearrange the way you look at things.

Such is the story of Mitch and Diane. Neighbors in a hip, up-and-coming community in Southern California, they became close friends. Diane was an attorney who often started work at the crack of dawn as she endeavored to make her way up the ladder of success. Mitch often bicycled by and dropped off coffee on his way to the travel agency he worked at down the street. They traded books, advice for broken hearts, and rides to the airport—the stuff of friendship. Easily, and without giving it much thought, they became threads in the fabric of each other's lives. Diane never took Mitch seriously as a potential beau because she thought he was kind of goofy, not reserved and self-important like the guys she was usually interested in. She could never understand why he didn't "grow up" and do something important with his life.

Then Diane decided to spend a year in Italy, working for the European branch of her firm. The man she was seeing had broken up with her, and she felt she needed to get away from her all-consuming job and spend a little more time taking in the sweeter side of things. So Diane packed up her life, took a tiny apartment in the oldest section of Rome, and began living "la dolce vita." Inspired by the antiquity and art all around her, Diane began to feel more alive than she had in a long while. She began to paint, to create passionate works that truly expressed her inner being. Diane found herself becoming less serious and more appreciative of the small pleasures in life: a good cup of coffee, a great conversation, or the laughter of children playing soccer in the street.

She had been in Rome for three months when Mitch stopped in to see her while on a bike tour through the neighboring countryside. She was excited to see her old friend; it was always fun to have someone from home to show around. As she approached his hotel, she saw Mitch standing outside in high-top Converse sneakers with his boyish grin, and suddenly his goofiness became the most charming thing she'd ever seen. "Our eyes met, and it all felt so different. Although he was the same old Mitch I'd always liked but sort of dismissed for being too undirected, all of a sudden he felt completely new and exciting to me. He seemed so cool and free-spirited." Diane gave him the Italian greeting of a kiss on each cheek, and they set off to see her newly adopted town. Days later, over an espresso at an outdoor café, they worked up the courage to talk about what they were feeling, which turned out to be nothing short of intense attraction. It turned into a deep love that lasted for the rest of Diane's year in Italy, and for twenty years of marriage to date.

"Mitch and I still talk about it to this day; we enjoy rehashing that transformative moment. Did it happen because I had awakened to my art? Did I need to go away in order to see things from a fresh perspective? Was it all just the timing? It felt to me like some sort of dramatic unveiling, like he was revealed to me when I was ready— a totally new awareness overcame me and changed the whole dynamic."

That sort of shift can be life altering. And it happens all the time. Soul mates are funny like that; they surprise us, catch us when we aren't looking, so that they can slip past the guards of our preconceptions. It's as if the soul—that part of us that is infinite and eternal—is always working to find the best way to draw us into situations that will wake us up to our potential.

In Diane's case, as soon as she got off the fast track to becoming a partner and let down her defenses by exploring a new life, she discovered that real love had been right there all along. And it's not uncommon for soul mates to show up when we stop searching for them and get on with our own lives, letting go of our expectations and projections. When Diane gave herself permission to enjoy her life, she also allowed Mitch to be who he was; more magnificent than she could ever have imagined.

Not all soul mates create the kind of steady, stable relationship that Mitch and Diane enjoy. Some soul mates can drag us kicking and screaming into our dark corners to finally face the so-called demons that hold us back from experiencing true love. They often bring things up for us which are unpleasant, sometimes pulling us right into the painful spaces we most want to avoid but need to address in order to become more fully integrated and enlightened.

I once dated a man who nearly destroyed me. He was both physically and emotionally abusive, but no matter how bad things got, I could not seem to leave. While we were together, all of the fears and insecurities I'd long since stuffed away came pouring out. I became a crazy person as I struggled through the dramas to avoid facing things I had never wanted to look at. Being with him triggered my hidden rage, my feelings of worthlessness, and my most manipulative and controlling behavior. I had always projected the image of being laid back and confident, but that man held my nose up to far less appealing aspects of myself until finally I had no choice but to do some deep inner work. The relationship, with all its heartbreak, inspired me to look at myself and figure out what needed to change. To this day, I remain grateful to him (from a respectful distance) and I count him as a soul mate. I would never return to him or wish to relive those times, but I know that by going through it all, a great healing occurred. My being drawn to him had divine purpose in it, and by staying in the game I became more conscious; the relationship woke me up in a sense. There are times we must make a decision to leave, yes; but usually that works best after we learn the lesson intended from the particular situation. Remember, if Spirit is omniscient and omnipresent, that means the ugly stuff has its place too; often it is the very stuff that brings us to critical breakthroughs necessary for growth and eventual happiness.

As you can see, soul mate love isn't always bliss and wonder; sometimes these are our most painful relationships, the ones that tear our hearts and test our mettle. Soul mate love shows us what we are made of and brings us more deeply into the realm of Spirit. Sometimes awareness comes through gentle recognition, and sometimes it storms into our world through pain. Each of us experiences the illumination in the manner most effective for us at that juncture in our life. The bad news (if you can call it that) is that the pain will keep coming back in somewhat the same form until we learn the lesson it is trying to bring; but the good news is that once we get it, that kind of dysfunction won't show up again.

We can't possibly know or dictate what will bring us our awakenings; no two people are exactly the same, and one soul certainly requires different lessons than the next. We simply have to rise to greet the occasions as they present themselves to us. Let me assure you right now that it *is* possible to be with someone for whom you care passionately and with whom you can sustain a loving, connected relationship. This is our goal. But in getting to that point there are challenges to be met. The perfect set of conditions for bringing about your soul's unfolding is always at hand, but you probably won't recognize this while you're going through it. The trick is to remain alert to the attraction and chemistry that presents itself to you so that you can discern what is being revealed in this, the divine curriculum of soul mate love.

A soul mate reflects back to us that which is unhealed while testifying to what is already perfect. Soul mates provide different things at different times: sometimes a safe haven from which we can branch out and explore, and sometimes challenges that bring us to our knees. In every case, they help us as we make our way along the path leading to the innermost sanctum where Spirit resides.

Ancestral Quest

Just as we are linked to our soul mates by what we need to learn, so we are connected to our ancestors by the tendencies they passed on to us. More than just blue eyes, diabetes, or musical abilities run in a family; so can a tendency toward bullish behavior, codependency, or holding grudges. Who we are is colored by where we came from. George Bernard Shaw said, "Life is no brief candle to me. It is a sort of splendid torch which I have got a hold of for the moment, and I want to make it burn as brightly as possible before handing it on to future generations." How our ancestors processed and dealt with life, and how successful they were at rising to their potential, significantly contributes to how we experience life. Each generation stands on the shoulders of the last, which means we have a responsibility to figure things out so that those who come after us will be bolstered by our successes rather than burdened by our shortcomings.

We are meant to become lighter, more conscientious beings; and so with each generation, there are new opportunities to push through plateaus reached by the ones who came before us. Even as they have strengthened our standing by their spiritual triumphs, our ancestors have also passed down to us unfinished business and challenges they could not rise to. These are systems of thought and behavior which need to be upgraded and perfected. By "herding" lessons through a family lineage, the soul can better refine—or streamline—an evolutionary trend.

Sometimes a shift in consciousness comes instantly and sometimes it takes many generations to occur. And so there are bits and pieces of generations past which flow through us like cellular memories and involuntary instincts. These memories and instincts are woven into us like a thread that connects us to the very first humans who moved away from the Source in order to expand and evolve. Moving away from the stillness of Source required a mindset which would separate out the "I" from the "All-that-is." Such was instilled in each of us as an entity called the ego. The ego can also be called free will or human nature. Because the ego was born with the mission to push out and separate from the Whole or Oneness, it naturally formed and continues to form gulfs, divisiveness, and divergent ideologies. In this manner, the story of humanity had lots of conflict and juice with which it could weave itself an ever-expanding new reality. People bumped up against each other as they made their way in the world, always doing the best they could to survive and thrive. But with each generation, with each new wave of experiences and level of awareness, humanity has evolved to become less primitive and more spiritually integrated. We moved away from God and now we are folding back in, enriched and enlightened and having increased "God-consciousness." Thus, our charge is to take what we have been given, what has been passed down to us, and integrate our divine nature into it so that we elevate the manner in which we occupy the planet. We are to appreciate what our forefathers handed down to us while at the same time polish the energy.

Because we are building on our ancestral heritage, it is quite likely that issues our parents unsuccessfully grappled with will show up to challenge us in our lives. We have been handed the story that they worked on, the story that was carried and worked on and handed over to them by their early influencers. Much of it is positive, but much of it still could stand an infusion of spiritual consciousness. And what we don't recognize as an area of growth to work on, the universe will designate for us. Life will show us in no uncertain terms where we need to develop.

If stoicism runs in your family, for instance, then life would likely try and teach you to open up and become more vulnerable. If tight-fisted control is the family stone, Providence would probably push you to learn the lesson of surrender. And if anger is something than ran unattended to throughout the history of your family, you would likely get lots of opportunities to heal unchecked anger. And by the way, just as brown hair or alcoholism can be passed down to one sibling and not the other, or even skip a generation, so can certain aspects of the family psyche end up with one person and not the other. You simply have to pay attention to what keeps showing up for you.

Although they may be frustrating, the difficulties and challenges are actually jumping-off points for enlightenment. Because they capture our attention in such a commanding way, they are major opportunities for growth. And because it is our nature to evolve spiritually, we will keep getting chances to achieve our potential, to realize our perfection. The miracle here is that when we do master what our forebears didn't, their souls are healed right along with ours. We have learned from physics that time and space are not fixed; they exist only as perceptions, as ways of organizing events in our world. So even though it might appear that your grandmother or great-grandmother is long since dead and gone, her soul keeps evolving. As one member of the family grows, all the others are affected and lifted as if by osmosis. Remember, we are all connected to each other by our divine heritage, so the fruits of our efforts are shared by everyone. We do great service to our ancestors—and our future progeny—when we take on issues that have yet to be dealt with.

And of course, who better than a soul mate to wake us up to where we need to grow? Here is how Tim and Judy tell the story of how they evolved out of some old family patterns:

Judy: "My parents always fought. Some families have the constant drone of television or the stereo as background, but we had Mom and Dad bickering—actually more like shouting—as the movie score of our lives. As I look back on it, the funny thing was that they both seemed to enjoy a good fight. It became almost a family sport to see who could get their opinions across emphatically enough to win the round. Even Grandma and Grandpa would join in. So when I started getting serious with Tim, the quiet in our lives was kind of unsettling. Alarming even."

Tim: "My family was the opposite of Judy's. My parents not only never raised their voices, but they never disagreed about anything, at least not in front of the kids. They always presented a united front, and we learned from a very early age not to challenge them. Around the dinner table there was always this feeling of 'don't rock the boat' as we made small talk and discussed only mundane things. We definitely learned to keep our problems to ourselves."

Judy: "Tim and I met at a record store. We were sampling the same CD and I just felt this electricity when he looked at me. I was so attracted to his calm and friendly smile that I asked him for his phone number. He looked pretty surprised, but he gave it to me. I sensed a gentleness about him that I was very drawn to. We fell in love very quickly; everything seemed to just click. We liked the same music, enjoyed hiking together, and both of us had similar goals for our lives. Everything was going along swimmingly until I started getting . . . almost scared. Like I didn't know how to do this. I found myself picking on him and starting fights. I would go into these tirades, and he would just hold me and try to quiet me down. And I have to admit, I enjoyed the added attention the drama brought; I started feeling plugged-in again.

"Looking back on it now, I can see that I didn't know

how to experience love without being a drama queen from time to time. I said mean things to Tim because I was trying to get a rise out of him, to inject some new life into our relationship, which had started feeling a little nicey-nice. I kept thinking he would fight back and then I could really show my stuff. But he didn't; he just withdrew from me."

Tim: "Then on Christmas of our second year of dating, we were with Judy's family at the dinner table and a war nearly broke out over the subject of politics. After my shock at how loud things got wore off—with the help of a couple glasses of wine—the situation became almost surreal to me. The barbs and jabs were sort of a show, and I realized this is how these people communicate. Even though I saw that they weren't altogether serious, I still felt uncomfortable and I remembered how in my family we were never allowed to disagree. I was tempted to walk right out of the house and never deal with Judy or her crazy family again. I didn't want what I grew up with, but neither did I want the insanity of Judy's family dynamic."

Judy: "Later that evening, Christmas Eve I think it was, Tim and I stayed up all night talking. Because I could see how hard it was for him to come out and say this stuff and because he didn't try to slam me with his opinions, I was able to listen openly to him as he pointed out how cruel my family could be to each other. Cruel? I had never thought we were cruel! But he told me about how I had hurt him from time to time with my remarks and insults, and for some reason I heard him that night. I really began to look at myself and the root of my behavior. I didn't want to thoughtlessly continue my family dynamic of screaming to be heard. I began to believe that love could be kind and calm—still passionate of course—just more considerate of each other's feelings."

Tim: "It was the most amazing Christmas, like some new understanding was born between us. It was hard for me to speak up and tell Judy I was hurt by her and that I disagreed with the way she and her family communicated. I really felt I was running the risk of losing her, but I didn't want to stay shut down anymore. Watching her riotous family sort of emboldened me to speak up (certainly not at the decibels they did) and state my case. It was a real leap for me. And I know it was a big thing for her to hear that sometimes she could be hurtful. But I was willing to change how I communicated, and I hoped she was too. It sounds corny, but I had a mental picture of us both walking on a high wire without a safety net, helping each other across."

Judy: "Now we meet somewhere in the middle. I try not to draw him into a fight, and Tim is so much more open about his thoughts and feelings. Both of us were challenged to go beyond our family patterns, and agreeing to give it a go was the best gift we could ever have given each other. I really do believe that we succeeded where our parents—God love 'em—just couldn't break the mold."

Let me be very clear here: breaking the mold does not mean turning away from your emotional legacy. Breaking the mold means *allowing* your attraction to a partner to take hold, *witnessing and experiencing* the difficulties that may come up with it, and then, with a solid intention to heal, *choosing* to do things with more awareness. This takes time, courage, and vulnerability; but it certainly pays off as the relationship deepens and matures due to the effort.

What makes Tim and Judy long-term soul mates is that they continue to be drawn to each other on many levels, and this pull is powerful enough that they hang in there when trouble arises. Both of them grew in leaps and bounds as a result of each bringing up the other's glitches. Judy was forced to address her identification with drama and Tim came face to face with his tendency to shut down. They may not have known how far back in the family history these tendencies went, but my guess is that they reached back far beyond just their parents. Tim and Judy really accomplished more than just making their relationship better; they evolved a whole pocket of energy that was ripe for enlightenment. This is one of the many faces of soul mate love!

* * *

Remaining observant and aware of what comes up for
you in a given situation is essential for fueling your spiritual enlightenment. I have found that introspective prayer
is quite helpful in this process, since it puts you in the
mindset of being a co-creator with God. Remember, we
are made up of both ego (self will) and Spirit, so we have
to integrate the two. The difference between a petitioning
prayer (God, can you please help my relationship to be
easier and make my wife aware that she is hurting me?)
and an introspective prayer (example following) is that
the former doesn't make you take responsibility, while the
latter really pushes you to see how you contribute to the
problem at hand. If you don't see how you are intricately
part of the problem, you render yourself powerless to
make a difference. So much of transcending old stuff requires that you recognize what is playing out; and once
you do, things can begin to shift. Here is an example of
how an introspective prayer might sound:

Ancestral Release Prayer

*As I breathe in I connect to Spirit. As I exhale I
sense my ego. My intention is to move through whatever blocks me; I sincerely desire healing and allow
it to come gently and with ease.*

In this moment I am witnessing anger as it arises when I think of my wife and how she berates me. I see how I am unwilling to stand up for myself for fear she will reject me. And I'm angry that I feel trapped by my need for her to stay.

I recall how Mom used to torture Dad like this, and here I am in the same conundrum. Still, I can't seem to let it go. Pit in my stomach. Jaw clenching. Skin crawling. Ok. I am breathing; I accept this. I surrender to this moment. And I welcome the presence of Spirit as I invite healing to occur.

I am seeing how sometimes I hide in the role of martyr or victim. I see what I get out of it in that I don't have to risk or work at changing myself. And I have to admit that I like how people feel sorry for me when I tell them about my situation.

I can shift this by committing to being more forthright with my needs and desires. I can stop telling people the details of our private life, thus disallowing the pity I had thrived on. I am willing to do things differently than my parents. My intention is to break new ground.

May I forgive with all my heart those who have hurt me. May I be forgiven by those who I have harmed. May this forgiveness extend to all my family members who have gone before me and will go after me. May there be peace in me and in those I love, now and always. Amen.

There is enormous power in witnessing what *is*. Simply by being aware of a dynamic, it can begin to shift. When we are unconscious of age-old patterns, they will continue to run our lives, but when we observe them objectively and see where fear traps us, healing can commence. We can get things moving by continuing to stay present and aware, always being willing to push ourselves past what may be comfortable. Growth is certainly not easy, but we are called on to face what our parents couldn't or wouldn't. It is up to us to gift our children—or the people we are close to—with cleaner slates and brighter energy; in this way, Spirit reaches through us to create a richer and more joyous universe.

Every day, in every encounter with another soul, we are given opportunities to break painful patterns and forge new ground. Romantic relationships are fertile gardens for growing into our higher selves. It's nearly impossible to do this kind of deep work alone; a soul mate relationship—crazy or gentle, loving or volatile, long-lasting or short-lived—provides an invaluable accelerant.

The Angel in Front of You

How do we know when the One has arrived? How can we know when to really get serious about our spiritual work? As my husband says, "If you wait too long for your ship to come in, your pier might collapse." Whoever is in your life right now is exactly who is supposed to be there. There are no mistakes, no wasted years; there are only the opportunities before you right now. Perhaps you've been wondering when the One will come along and rescue you from a relationship that seems to offer nothing exciting. Or perhaps you are stuck in a dance of drama, hoping against hope that things will miraculously smooth themselves out. Or maybe there doesn't seem to be anyone significant at all. Well, here is something important to understand: *until you can see and honor the innocence and perfection of the one who stands before you, you will not be able to perceive the full glory of love at its greatest.* Love is like a skill we have to practice; we need to learn to love whoever is in our life right now. And if there isn't anyone you think is the One, learn to love a friend, a family member, or even a shopkeeper whom you barely know just so you can get your spiritual muscles working. Often, we are clouded by our judgments and don't even see the potential staring us right in the face. We either see someone as a person to brace ourselves against or we see them as someone to whom we want to extend our kindness, open heart, and good will.

Take one person (let's call him Al) as seen by two different people (let's call them Sandy and Liza). Sandy has a suspicious nature, so she expects that people always have something up their sleeves—an agenda. After an hour at dinner with Al, she notices him checking his watch and figures he probably has a rendezvous with another woman and is trying to cut short their time together. Seeing him as sneaky and untrustworthy, she stops engaging in the conversation, and begins giving very short responses. Sandy has braced herself against Al, thinking he is a typical man who wants to use her or take her for granted.

When Liza is at dinner with Al and he checks his watch, she hardly notices, but the sight reminds her to check her watch too. She realizes it's getting late. They decide to pay the check and walk home, laughing at the fact that both of them are early birds. Liza is reassured by Al's directness and finds she has enjoyed herself and the evening immensely.

Sandy, because of her suspicious nature, distanced herself from someone who could have been fun and interesting. Liza, because of her assumption of Al's goodness, felt connected and found a potential mate.

The truth is that what we believe is usually what we see. The writer Anais Nin keenly observed, "We don't see things as they are, we see them as we are." By our interpretation of people, we either move away or move closer to an awareness of love. Quite often, though, our beliefs are unconscious; we may not realize we are suspicious or angry or pessimistic. Once again, these internal glitches

will be teased out of us by a partner (or romantic interest) so that we can confront and heal them.

Here is a questionnaire to see how you tend to view
the world. Answer the following as honestly as you can.

Summing up the Person in Front of You

1. Do you see people, for the most part, as good
   or bad?
2. Do you tend to trust what people say, and does
   your opinion usually end up being correct?
3. Do you immediately zero in on a person's
   flaws, or are you more likely not to notice a
   wrinkle, or bad grammar, or what a person's
   wearing?
4. Do you find yourself only relating to a specific
   type of person, or are you more open to diverse
   experiences?
5. Do you withhold your kindness if someone
   doesn't "fit the bill"?
6. Do you tend to see innocence or guilt?
7. Do you expect someone to make you feel good,
   and if they don't, turn away from them?

If you go with your initial gut reaction when answering these questions, you will begin to see how you perceive and interact with people. Unless you see everyone

as having equal and distinct value, you are not operating from your highest spiritual potential. And if you are not operating from your highest potential, you will not resonate with the highest potential of soul mate love. What shows up outside of us is a reflection of what is going on inside. Of course we can't give equal time and energy to everyone—and not everyone will want it—but we *can* realize that each and every person has Spirit within them, partners included. We *can* treat people with dignity, respect, and benevolence no matter who they are. And if we aren't doing that, we are the ones who are missing out.

When we judge people for how "important" or "right" they are, we overlook the gifts they bear for us. By focusing on someone's flaws we limit our experience of them. And that's what happens between people every day, at every moment. Either we invite them to show us their greatness, the Spirit within them, and we grow from that exposure, or we refuse their potential by noticing only what is wrong. It's up to us: we benefit or suffer according to the lens we choose to use.

If I am at a party and I think everyone there is dull and not worth my time, I will most likely have missed a brilliant conversation with someone who needed only the slightest opening from me before launching in. *Everyone* has something to offer. Everyone has a story to tell, and through our stories we connect at the most meaningful level of Spirit. And once we set aside our judgments, all sorts of surprises begin to show up. I can't tell you how many people, after they have done their inner work and learned to temper their judgments, have told me, "I never would have imagined that I would end up with someone who was extroverted [or shy, or bald, or lived in Tokyo]." You cannot know what the universe has in store for you, and clinging to a particular vision of how your soul mate should be can only limit the opening through which he or she will appear.

It may not be ours to dictate *who* comes into our lives, but we certainly have a choice about how to perceive and interact with them. According to that discernment, we will either move forward or stay stuck. We invite in more love when we see the world around us through loving eyes, and we entertain isolation or hostility when we look through the lens of judgment. It's really up to us. Relationships serve as a wonderful mirror to show us just how we are doing and spur us on to further growth.

At every moment, in every split second, Spirit is revealed or Spirit is concealed. When we see the person before us as lovable, Spirit is revealed, because, as we know from every spiritual tradition, the fundamental truth is that Spirit (or love) underlies everything. On the other hand, when we see the person before us as unlovable, we miss an opportunity to perceive from our highest and most God-like abilities. In God's eyes, we are all perfect. As was said by thirteenth century mystic, Yunus Emre, in

The Drop That Became the Sea, "Those whom the Beloved loves, we must also love."

This is not to say you shouldn't pay attention when you are hurt or angry at someone's behavior and express yourself in a responsible way. Do allow yourself to experience whatever feelings arise, and then choose to be loving in the most appropriate way. Of course, we need not hang around for something that is abusive or harmful; being loving starts with taking care of ourselves. But we serve ourselves well by recognizing that whoever stands before us—be it husband, girlfriend, criminal, or boss—is a manifestation of Spirit. They may seem benign or menacing, but we are all, at our center, made of the very same stuff. We are all the individualized presence of God, helping to weave the fabric of constant creation; our choices on how we interact with each other will dictate what the world will grow into.

Magic takes place when you really absorb the knowledge that we are all in this together. The soul's inclination is to reunite, bringing together our diversity to enrich the ever expanding Whole; the ego works to separate and polarize. Our greatest spiritual undertaking, then, is to replace judgment with empathy. The more we are able to interpret "bad" behavior as a call for help, the less angry and victimized we will feel in the face of it. Through the force of our compassion—by putting ourselves in each other's shoes—divisiveness can be overcome. We will come to know a sense of empowerment and freedom as we leave behind the fears that support old patterns of negativity and instead move with all our heart to embody a more evolved way of relating.

We can only move in one direction at a time. (Try to walk forward and step back at the same time; it's impossible.) In much the same way, it is impossible to act lovelessly and still move in the direction of joy. We simply can't do both. As tempting as it is to assess your partner—or potential partner—as inadequate, every time you do, you limit your own experience of love. Does this mean we are required to love everyone, despite their behavior? Ultimately, yes. Does it mean we have to go on a date, commit to them, or share a life together? No. But you are to realize that any person with whom you have a spark of connection is an angel presenting an opportunity to transmute your lower instincts and rise to mastery. Once you comprehend this, things become very clear. We are here to learn how to love and be loved, and everything is perfectly coordinated to bring that about.

Some Native Americans have a powerful practice that calls for living "with death on your shoulder." If death could come at any time, then every moment is sacred. If you knew you were going to die soon, would you see the person before you differently? Might you connect with a word, or a touch, or the sparkle in your eye and send them into their day a little happier for having been with you? Indeed you would. You wouldn't care what position they held in life. It wouldn't matter if they were over-weight or well-dressed. In the face of imminent death, things get very simple and very lucid. We want to know we have touched and affected someone. We want to ex-perience our capacity for love; this is our spiritual man-date. And whoever stands before us gives us that very opportunity.

We need the challenge relationships provide by calling us out on our prejudices, and we need people—partners, friends, casual acquaintances, and even strangers—who will walk with us as we make our way to our soul's po-tential. And only by behaving as if each and every person we come in contact with is an angel sent directly from God can we transcend our small self in favor of the big Self. Difficult, to say the least; and yet we find in these relationships the perfect training ground for our intimacy with Spirit.

True love arrives unsolicited when the mind is without judgment, when we wholly accept ourselves and those around us. When we see each person, and especially our partner, as an angel come to awaken us from our sleep, we can begin to sense the proximity of the One.

chapter three

Obstacles

". . . that great nature in which we rest . . . that Unity, that Over-Soul, within which every man's particular being is contained and made one with all other . . . We live in succession, in division, in parts, in particles. Meantime within man is the soul of the Whole; the wise silence; the universal beauty, to which every part and particle is equally related; the eternal One."
—RALPH WALDO EMERSON, *ESSAYS*

Love is always present, always available to us, but we just don't see it sometimes. It's like the car keys we search for everywhere, only to discover they were sitting on the front hall table all the time. In much the same way, fulfillment awaits discovery right under our noses, but it is veiled from our awareness. For many reasons—most of them unconscious—we hold ourselves back from contentedness. Even though we direct so much of our energy into finding and sustaining the ideal relationship, it can seem to elude us. But it's not that love is dodging us, or even holding out until we become worthy of it; instead we hold ourselves back from experiencing love. We crouch behind the walls and close the gate to our heart.

We turn love away when we hang on to old behaviors and beliefs based on fear and distrust. Those old patterns are like obstacles that keep us from a soulful relationship. Our charge, then, is to familiarize ourselves with the internal terrain of our defense mechanisms so that we can dismantle them. We can only go so far by superficial tinkering; if we want fundamental change, a major overhaul is required. But don't worry, it's not as daunting as it sounds; it's just a matter of educating yourself to recognize the hiccups in your system so that you can reconfigure things. Once the way is made clear, love will come rushing in.

Ego

There are so many ways to interpret the word *ego*. Usually it describes someone's conceit or grandiosity. But it is also an aspect of our mind that legendary psychologist Sigmund Freud said is our conscious experience of who we are in the world. His younger colleague, Carl Jung, went on to say that it is the center of the conscious part of the psyche. All of this is true, valid, and far more complex than I am explaining; but for the purpose of talking about the ego in a spiritual context, we can simplify things by saying it is the instinctive part of us that looks out for "me, mine, and my way." It is that part of us that, as the Buddhist nun and author Pema Chodrin put it, ". . . resist[s] our complete unity with all of life, resisting the fact that we change and flow like the weather, that we have the same energy as all living things . . ." In other words, the ego is that part of us that declares and works to preserve a sense of separation from each other. It is the aspect of the mind that demands attention, cultivates desires, and tries to survive by wielding power and manipulation.

The ego is unaware that we are part of a larger whole. Because the ego identifies with the "I" (separation) rather than the "we" (unity), it stays very busy trying to make sure everything goes its way. Its sole (fear-based) purpose is to maintain survival in what it perceives to be threat or competition in anything or anyone outside of itself. The ego remains oblivious to the fact that when one of us thrives, all of us thrive; it is always working to achieve dominance and safety in a limited world. You know you are operating out of an egoic place when the backdrop of your thoughts has more to do with serving yourself rather than relaxing into the rhythm of ever abundant Spirit.

I am not suggesting that all things that come from ego are bad; the ego was instilled in us for a reason. If not for ego, we would not have all the dramas in life which coax from us growth and expansion. And certainly we need not relinquish all our individuality, all aims and desires. It's just that if we are to tap into to our spiritual power and experience more love, we would do well in terms of our evolution to *lean toward* a way of being that relies more on intuition than on intellect, more on compassion than on external manipulation, more on love than on fear. Intellect and ego are essential to getting along in the world, and even fear is useful at times to promote survival; but these need not be the overriding energies of our lives.

A woodsman friend of mine once told me the story of a hiker who got lost in a forest on a cloudy night. The ranger had given him an outdated map, and after hours of taking wrong turn after wrong turn, the hiker found himself deep in the woods with no clue on which way to go. He had already spent the better part of six hours trying to recall where he had misstepped, hoping that if only he could put all the pieces together in his mind, he would be able to methodically make his way back to camp. He had no compass, no knowledge of the stars, and there was no one around to help him. Every frantic move he made seemed to put him farther away from where he wanted to go.

Finally, he concluded that being panicked was getting him nowhere. So he found a little outcropping of rocks and sat atop the highest one and closed his eyes. He forced himself to do some deep breathing until his nerves settled down and, for a few moments, rested in the mystery and beauty around him. Almost instantly, a calm overtook him and he knew he would be OK. He decided to hunker down for the night and sleep in a little crevice between the rocks, which would serve to shield him from the weather and any curious animals. He awoke the next morning to a clear sky and industriously went about making an S.O.S. from the branches in the surrounding area. Sure enough, a search helicopter flew over and saw his call for help and the hiker was rescued.

My point in retelling this story is to illustrate that the hiker's ego could not get him out of the woods. Had he dwelt on his fury at being given the wrong information, he would likely have perished a "righteous" man. Had he persisted in trying to do things "his way," he would have come up short, because he was not an astute person when it came to directions. Instead, he got quiet, and in the silence of his quiet mind, he became inspired—almost assured—that things would be all right as the plan popped into his thinking. By relaxing into a more calm and connected state of mind, he began to feel at one with the world around him; the hiker tapped into a "knowingness" of how to be and what to do. He was no longer resistant to his situation, nor was he bullish to get what he wanted. Instead, he became submissive to a larger intelligence.

To get to that knowingness—that feeling of *at-one-ness* that opens us to intuition or insight—the ego must be calmed down and quieted. If we want to make room for the divine to take the lead in our lives, the hysteria of the ego must not be indulged; we have to put it aside so the answers can come.

We all *know* things when we tap into this divine stillness. Our connectedness with nature, with each other, and with God is the source of our own creative wisdom; it is the energy that helps us move through obstacles and elevates our experience of life. And when we connect to Spirit, or the divine mind within us, we automatically connect to Spirit within another. In relationships, the tamping down of the ego can be witnessed in more kindness and consideration toward each other. We become more generous and less competitive as we learn to allow things to be as they are.

To get to this peaceful state, we must consciously deflate the ego. We have to tell our desire to control things to settle down and let the greater force of Spirit within us become the primary driver of what we do and say. This doesn't mean we won't count on our intelligence to make rational decisions and sort through options and dilemmas. And it doesn't mean we can't use our ego to pump ourselves up with the confidence necessary to get something specific accomplished. It's just that it is extremely important not to let the ego overextend its domain.

In working with clients, I find that the most difficult stance for people to assume is one of being relaxed and simply allowing things to be as they are. It's not easy to let go and trust that everything will work out as it should. You will find yourself saying things like, "Sure, that sounds nice, but you can't just 'let go' when you are in New York City hunting for a parking space, and you certainly can't just allow your partner free rein. Sometimes you have to *push* your agenda or you'll never get what you want."

But consider how my friend David applied the principle of "letting go" to the nearly impossible task of parking in New York City on the days he drove down from Woodstock. He found that when he was in a pure and relaxed state of mind, his ego (control, agenda, self-centered will) firmly in the backseat, parking spaces would seem to materialize as he cruised by in his big, clunky pickup truck. As if choreographed, as soon as he pulled up to where he needed to go, someone would be leaving. It may sound crazy, but David's good parking karma makes perfect sense when we recall that all matter is just energy. The energy around us simply responds to the energy within us. Resistance begets resistance, and openness begets openness. If we lead with ego, we will draw to us even more struggle; when we drop our need to direct how things will work out, they just manifest with ease.

Our spiritual task is to calm our overactive ego, to catch it when it starts climbing into the driver's seat and tell it to get back where it belongs. In terms of love relationships, we need to become more focused on treating our partners—or potential partners—with respect, honoring the fact that they have their own higher mind to follow and we have no right to push our personal agenda on their lives. We need to stop insisting on getting our way and allow them to be who they are. We can make suggestions and we can express our opinions, but it gets us nowhere to *insist* on having things our way. We can't change anyone else; we can only work on changing ourselves.

Power struggles are a major problem in love relationships, and I have found that whenever a power struggle develops between partners, at least one of the following aspects of ego is at work: 1. the need to be right; 2. the need to be in control; 3. the need to be distracted; or 4. the need to feel superior or inferior. Let's look at these more closely, for each of them calls for achieving a healthier balance.

The **need to be right** pits us against each other. When we are attached to being right, we feel compelled to defend ourselves at all costs. We don't want to see the other person's side of the story, because if we did, it might threaten the case we've built. So we dig in our heels, hoping to wear the other person down. We do this because deep down inside we feel small and afraid. The ego believes only one of us can win, so it is fighting for its life.

If we were to take a more spiritual approach and recognize that the Spirit in me is the same as the Spirit in you, we would no longer need to be right. Rather than fearfully clinging to our smaller, more selfish agenda, we could shift our goal to finding *common ground.*

When I catch myself vehemently making my point, it's usually because I'm bullying my way through a situation that I'm worried could hurt me. I've finally come to the realization that when we slow down and listen deeply with an open heart, *everyone* has a valid point. And if one of us can back off and give the other some breathing room, the other person will usually come around to the same realization.

Believe me, I can fight with the best of them. But does winning make me happy? No. And it certainly doesn't make for an open and communicative relationship. Now when disagreements arise, I remind myself to move toward deep listening rather than trying to win. In this way, my heart opens rather than shuts down. It's difficult sometimes, and I have to force my ego to get out of the way, but when I make an effort to see the other side of things, the struggle seems to soften and unwind.

The **need to be in control** is the ego's way of urging us to hold tightly to the reins if we want to be safe. We'd better put things in their place, including our partners, says the fearful voice inside us. When I get into control mode, it's usually because I am scared that things won't work out as I think they should, and that, at the end of the day, I won't be okay.

I remember a long time ago trying to get a guy I was dating to commit to me. I started dropping all sorts of hints, reading him magazine articles about how men were healthier and happier when they were married. I tried playing mind games by alternately making him jealous and threatening that he would lose me if he didn't step up, then playing the part of the perfect girlfriend and fawning all over him. I did everything I could to get that man to do what I wanted him to do. I would have small successes, but his heart was never in it. Finally I recognized that all my manipulations were getting me nowhere. So I threw my ego out of the driver's seat and I surrendered the relationship to Spirit. For a while, once the pressure was off, my boyfriend wanted me like never before. But before long we both came to realize we weren't right for each other, and we broke up. As hard as it was to let go of the reins at the time, the absolute right thing happened once I did. I moved on, as did he, and we both met and married soul mates. I'm not saying that I give up control unflinchingly now, or that things go perfectly when I do, but every time I set aside my ego's tendency to control things, whatever obstacles were in my way seem to miraculously disappear.

The **need to be distracted** is the ego's way of coping with the anxiety of going it alone. There is a tremendous amount of fear and pressure that goes with the belief that you have to figure everything out for yourself. When the responsibility becomes too much, the ego looks for distraction; it is a way of surviving. And in our society, there is no shortage of distraction from the deeper issues of our humanity. Sensational news, demanding work schedules, lifestyle pressures, sports events, e-mail, computer games: these are just a few of the stimuli that compete for our attention. And trumping all of these is the drama we can create in our relationships; nothing beats a good knock-down drag-out fight to get our mind off the gnawing fear that we can't keep it all together. When we sweat the small stuff, we successfully distract ourselves from the larger anxiety that the ego maintains of being separate and alone in a big, scary world.

In other words, you may make a big deal about your husband coming home an hour later than he said he would, or lay into your wife for not running the household as well as you think she should, but really, deep down inside, you are just trying to distract yourself from the absolute terror of not being able to keep all the pieces of your life together. But you see, we are not meant to hold it all together; we are not the glue of life. Spirit is. We are at our best when we accept our role as *co*-creators with Spirit.

I usually find myself becoming a drama queen when I get anxious that I have taken on more than I can handle. When I start to feel that I don't really have what it takes to succeed, I start picking at little things so I can avoid a full-blown depression about the big stuff that seems too difficult to broach. But sometimes a full-blown depression (or breakdown) is what is required to free us of the belief that we are the sole creators of our lives. Sometimes we need to be reminded that by surrendering to Spirit, the perfect answers and solutions will come.

The **need to be superior or inferior** is the ego's way of keeping us apart from each other by focusing on flaws. It plagues us with attacks of self-pity or delusions of grandeur that keep us from the fundamental truth that we are all created equally and from the same source. Because the ego has no awareness of our inherent Oneness, it sets us adrift on our narcissistic wanderings. Our sense of worth should never depend upon how much better or worse we are doing than someone else. Rather, it should be rooted in the knowledge that we are all created perfectly by God.

There are times when I feel vastly inferior to my husband. He is very knowledgeable about history, business, and world affairs. I don't take in and retain that sort of information like he does, and if I'm not careful, I can start feeling inadequate during our marathon dinner conversations. If I remain unconscious of my fear of not being enough, I can become defensive to cover up my feeling small.

On the other hand, there are times when I feel I tower above him on subjects of literature or philosophy or psychology, and I can't believe that he doesn't understand what seems to be second nature to me. Here, again, I run the risk of giving into my ego (this time by feeling superior) if I don't see that we each have our areas of expertise and we enrich each other by filling in each other's spaces. I have to remember that I am enhanced by someone else's brilliance, not diminished by it, and that the same holds true for my partner. I have unique and wonderful things to offer, just as you do. My ego would have me feeling competitive, but if I catch it in the act I can adjust my thinking according to the spiritual principles of equality and all inclusiveness.

These four ego-driven needs present obstacles to our awareness of deep and unconditional love because they keep us focused on what's wrong rather than what's right. They drive us apart rather than bring us together. Each time you see one of these needs arise in your thoughts or actions, recognize it as a warning to relegate the ego to the backseat.

Ego may present us with many pitfalls, but it also has its benefits. It assists us in recognizing and celebrating our differences. We are unique, after all, and this uniqueness works in concert with our core spirituality. As we learn to coexist and enjoy the different qualities we all have, Spirit is renewed and expanded. Life becomes more textured and lovely.

The question is not whether the ego is good or bad, but rather to what degree we allow it to rule our lives and relationships. Ego is an aspect of the mind that serves a purpose; we just can't let it get out of hand. If we keep choosing to stay alert and awake to all the forces at work within us, we can create a well-balanced and soulful partnership.

The Dark Voice

Isn't it uncanny how our partners can sometimes push our buttons like no one else? They seem to be able to drive us crazy in ways we never even imagined. At those times, we want nothing more than to escape, or to attack with everything in our arsenal. It's as if something dark within us takes over and demands to be reckoned with.

Carl Jung introduced the idea of the shadow as an archetype (a pattern of thought that exists in all of us); he described it as our dark side, the unconscious part of us that houses all the raw thoughts and desires we are ashamed to admit to. This part of our psyche contains those aspects of our character that—thanks to a disapproving society, shaming parent, or strict religious ethos— we cannot acknowledge or act out. Because when we were very young we received the message that these traits were bad, we repressed or denied them. To our conscious mind, these inadmissible parts of our self ceased to exist. In their place we developed a mask, a more pleasing and acceptable front to present to the world.

In *A Little Book on the Human Shadow,* poet Robert Bly elaborated on this theme by saying that we were all born with a personality that expressed the entirety of our human nature without restriction. As we grew up, we were taught that certain parts of ourselves (sexuality, confidence, anger, impishness, etc.) were deplorable. So somewhere deep inside we made a decision not to be that way anymore. Bly says it was as if we stuffed into a bag all those undesirable pieces of ourselves, which we then had to lug around—hidden—for the rest of our lives. In therapeutic terms, we *disowned* a significant part of who we are.

Jung tells us that once we reintegrate the shadow, we can use all those suppressed aspects to unlock our creativity and to access our higher Self. And by tapping into our higher Self, all things become possible. By making peace with what we thought was so ugly in us, we bring peace to our relationship, and also into the world. Clearly, tending to the shadow is important work.

But how do we face what we've buried away and cannot see? And if we can't see it, how can we heal it? This is part of the brilliance inherent in relationships: *we spot in our partners what we have disowned in ourselves.* If someone is annoying in a way that evokes an irrational or over-the-top reaction in you, chances are good that they are reflecting back to you something from your own dark side. One of the clues that points to the shadow being projected is the level of emotion that gets aroused; it's one thing to be irritated, but if something your partner—or person of interest—does gets under your skin to an extent that is blown way out of proportion, you have likely stumbled into the arena of shadow. Instead of trying to change that person's behavior, though, you would do well to see it as a valuable sign of something that needs to be acknowledged, forgiven, and healthfully reintegrated *in you*.

Let's look more closely at this dynamic. If you are in a relationship and cannot stand your partner's neediness, for instance, I would suggest that perhaps you are needy yourself, but are ashamed of it. If you really hate your partner's bad temper, you might consider that you have anger *within you* that you aren't comfortable with. If you can't bear seeing your partner being playful, look within to see if there isn't a playful side to you that has been put down and locked away. Quite probably, when we isolate what it is we loathe about our partner, we will be awakened to what we have demonized in ourselves.

Try as you might to change the aspect of your partner that really gets under your skin, it will remain. In fact, if you are not making the connection that it has something to do with you, it will seem to get worse. So listen to the voice in your head that rants about your partner's failing and assume it is a *direct communication from your wounded and disowned self* intended to help you reintegrate and heal yourself.

What I call the Dark Voice is the communiqué from the

shadow that leads us into those places where we feel broken and wounded. It is like the S.O.S. signal saying, "Here I am! Please listen to me! I am stuck down here and I need some help." The voice of the shadow calls you to the spiritual and emotional aspects you need to integrate in order to become healthy, whole, and joyful. It brings your attention to that which you do not want to face, but must. It calls your attention to fear, shame, despair, or rage—states of mind that hold you back from loving and being loved.

Here is a meditation to acquaint you with your Dark Voice. By allowing yourself to hear it, you can follow it like a homing device to the suppressed feelings that hold your soul in bondage.

Dark Voice Meditation

Breathe deeply and slowly with your eyes closed, centering yourself. Feel the presence of Spirit within and all around you, holding you safely in a place of total openness.

Hold your partner's image in your mind and allow your opinions and issues to float to the surface. Notice the thoughts that hold a charge. Breathe into them.

Listen to the Dark Voice that arises. What does it say? Listen for the emotions that are revealing them-

selves, and allow them to be expressed fully. Instead of pushing away what is uncomfortable, move toward it, being completely attentive to what comes up. Instead of judging, simply allow it all to be.

Ask the Voice to tell its story of how your original pain—now being reflected by your partner—came to pass.

Feel compassion for what you've been through. Now visualize the light of Spirit healing any and all repercussions from the wound. Listen to the Dark Voice as its tone begins to lighten in gratitude for being allowed to speak.

Feel the healing at work in your psyche, reintegrating the banished pieces into a new wholeness.

When you feel you have heard all that you need to, take three deep breaths and open your eyes.

By performing this meditation, you have initiated the process of making peace with your so-called demons. You have begun to pull together your scattered self so that you can rediscover your deeper truth and power. You will come across things you might not understand; you will find things about yourself you have a hard time accepting; but this is your challenge. You are to replace fear with love. You are to accept yourself without judgment. When I went through my own dark night of the soul, I found this work extremely helpful in clarifying why I was stuck. I did the above meditation and the following exercise many, many times over about a six-month period. It was intense work, and sometimes I found myself screaming and raging, while at other times I curled up on the sofa and wailed until the wave of emotion passed. It always did pass, I am grateful to report, and eventually the way I related to myself and others changed in miraculous ways because I was no longer projecting my disowned stuff. Of course things still come up for me, and when they do, I break out this work and I do it all again. But things tend to move more swiftly through me now, as if much of what was in the bag has already been spread out on the table and looked at. I definitely carry a lighter load.

Take some time with the following exercise. I recommend you do it in a place that is completely private. If you can't find it at home, get into your car and drive to an empty parking lot or someplace where you can be alone. Actually, a closed car can be a perfect soundproof healing venue! Before you begin, say a little prayer for this process to be guided and protected by Spirit. State your intention to heal, that what comes up is not meant to indulge that part of you which is stuck, but instead loosen up and reverse its negative charge. And then call up all those disowned bits of yourself and give them a chance to make some noise.

Dark Voice Integration Work

1. Call to mind what is currently driving you crazy about your partner and note where that quality is actually hidden within you.

2. Listen to the Dark Voice as it begins to vent.

3. Allow its shadow energy to express itself through you. Scream, cry, rage; take your time in allowing the wounded self to become known and heard.

4. Try to remember the moment you decided it was not okay to be who you were.

5. Every time you get embarrassed at what is coming up, breathe deeply into the shameful energy and let it take you as far as it needs to go. It won't last more than a few minutes, so let it carry you.

6. Listen to your inner voice and to your body as they bring to the surface what lies hidden within.

7. You will sense a natural winding-down or even a click of completion in the process, and as you do, witness all the feelings that have come up and have compassion for them.

8. Forgive yourself, and in that forgiveness, feel the lightness of Spirit moving through your entire being.

9. When you feel ready (but not until you authentically feel ready), forgive the person or
people who caused you to shut down.

10. Address the part of you that was wounded
with the voice of your Higher Power. Assure it
that all is well and that love is present now.

11. Feel gratitude for the cleansing work you have
accomplished, knowing that the peace you've
made is real and lasting.

12. Return to the work as often as it takes to get
to the point where there is no longer a charge on
a particular quality or issue. It might take three
sessions, and it might take thirty; have patience.

As you do this work it will become clear that you did
the best you could at the time of the original wound. You
will learn that the Dark Voice is a guide that can lead you
into and through the most hidden terrain of your psyche.
You might discover that you have a lot of anger and be
concerned that a spiritual person should not be an angry
one. But anger, like any emotion, is only harmful if you
hang on to it or act out on it irresponsibly. If you simply
listen to it with an ear toward healing it, you can let it go.
By allowing yourself the freedom to accept yourself
wholly, you will come to forgive and have compassion for
yourself and others. When this occurs, one of three things
will happen: your partner will, seemingly out of nowhere,

stop doing what was driving you crazy; it will cease to bother you; *or* the relationship will fall away altogether because it no longer resonates with your newfound sense of peace and acceptance. This cannot help but happen, since energy, just like water, seeks its own level.

In addition to doing Dark Voice work, I have found that it is sometimes necessary to do some sort of psychotherapeutic work at various times during one's life. Occasionally we need to hear an outside voice reflecting on what we say about ourselves and our feelings. Sometimes we cannot see our neuroses and we simply need help. It's one thing to be present and aware, but another to process memories or traumas without guidance. Concrete feedback can help to push us past the stuck places. You can get this help by turning to a trusted confidant or member of the clergy if therapy isn't a financial option. There are also many kinds of support groups and counseling centers that offer services as well.

Relationship Idolatry

When we expect another human being to make us happy or heal us of our woes, we put them on a pedestal and look to them to be our saviors. We do this with love relationships also, singling them out as the most important thing to make life good and fulfilling. We all too often look to our partnerships to define us and focus on them in hopes of filling the empty hole inside us, which can only be filled by a connectedness to Spirit.

Admittedly, some of the most powerful experiences of Spirit come through the vessel of a romantic relationship, but that doesn't mean we should pursue romance at the expense of developing and nurturing our own inner life. Relationship idolatry happens when we place too much emphasis on our relationship rather than working on our own Self-realization. What you might think you should get from a relationship—a sense of peace, love, and security—is really only attainable by getting in touch with your spiritual nature. I know of many people in relationships who, despite their romantic involvement (or involvements), continue to find these emotional states elusive; this is because they depend on the fantasy that someone should be "everything" to them. But relationships cannot take the place of Spirit; they can only serve to show us the way to it.

Being in love and enjoying all that romance has to offer is a wonderful gift. But we can't possibly know real joy if we look to conditions outside of ourselves for the cause. Because the purpose of life is to grow and become ever more intimate with God, we will be continuously disappointed by the ego's promise of external fulfillment until we finally get frustrated enough to consider another possibility. Being "let down" by partnership, then, is one of those blessings in disguise. If we are let down often and hard enough, we might stop pinning our dreams on an impossibility and instead begin to wake up to our Self— that core aspect of ourselves that is Spirit.

Much as we may bemoan the insufficiencies of our relationship (or lack thereof), that disappointment can motivate us to look deeper. We may keep looking to other people for a while, hoping against hope that there is someone else out there who can provide us with what we need, but eventually we will give up. "Giving up" has a negative connotation; it reads like failure, or loss, or weakness. But the kind of giving up I am speaking of is an act of surrender to our Higher Power, or Spirit, or God. When we have exhausted our personal effort and still don't have the joy we want, we can turn to the divine for intervention and guidance. That's when miracles happen. The moment we give up the idea that love is something to find *out there* is the moment it comes flooding into our awareness.

It is inevitable that we will awaken to who we are; how long that awakening takes depends upon how tightly we cling to the idea that a soul mate should be the be-all and end-all. We might be ushered into awareness by noticing that romance no longer has the ability to cheer us up, or we might be shocked into it when our partner leaves us for someone else and we are left to wonder why. Imagine that Spirit stands right before you, but your gaze is fixed on who might come around the corner. What a tragedy, what a missed opportunity, and yet we do it all the time. We only see the idol we worship, and thus Spirit—real love—remains concealed until we open ourselves to it. The bigger picture *includes* the love of a partner but does not depend upon it. We limit ourselves when we put so much pressure on a relationship to be something it cannot be.

Exercise for Identifying the Idol

Here is a chance to explore what you really believe. Take your time and listen closely to your inner voice to see which basket you put your eggs in.

1. I want to be with my soul mate because

_____.

2. I believe this person can change the way I feel by _____.

3. My soul mate would be different from my current partner in that _____

_____.

4. Life with my soul mate would be different in that _____.

5. I would like to shine, but I can't because

_____.

6. I would be happy if _____

_____.

7. I am delivered from my pain by

_____ .

8. My partner always makes me _____

_____ .

Are you giving your power away to the false idol of "relationship"? Are you dependent on another for your fulfillment? We put our well-being in a precarious position when we worship at the feet of romance. Romance is lovely; it is a thing to be enjoyed and learned from. But it is a means to an end (really an endless end). It is not the answer. It is only one of the pathways back to our Self.

Only by coming from your true spiritual nature will you find real and lasting peace, and only by acting in ways that testify to love will you come to know Spirit. If you are looking to a false god, you simply won't find the love you seek. The very nature of seeking implies that you don't believe you already have what you're looking for, and implicit in that is a sense of lack, emptiness. When you project lack, lack is reflected back to you; you manifest what you believe. Enduring soul mates love each other deeply, but they do not live as though everything was supplied by this one other person. If they were to lose that one person, would their happiness be doomed to disappear forever? Of course not.

Relationship idolatry is a form of spiritual laziness: we

need not do deep work if we are reaching for a superficial salve. If I can be with someone who brings excitement into my life, for instance, I don't have to look at why my life is not exciting. I don't have to challenge myself or push myself to grow. Rather than taking a leap into the vast unknown of our potential, we look to a partner. Instead of cultivating those aspects of ourselves that are underdeveloped, we turn to someone else to complete us. Truly though, limitless happiness can be found within each of us; it is there for the asking. If you are unable to look to yourself and your interconnectedness with all of life around you as the source of joy, you may miss out on your own potential glory and the gifts God instilled in you.

A partner can inspire us to see things differently. But they can't *be* the light that keeps us aglow. We need Spirit for that. We must move purposefully to get past our obstacles to Spirit. We have to find our own joy by *being* joyful. We have to find our own excitement by *being* exciting. We have to find our own love by *being the very love we seek*. All these things are possible when we ask God to assist and guide us.

We can have fine lives looking to our partners for love; we can surely get bits and pieces and glimpses of the real thing. But we can have *magnificent and miraculous* lives should we decide to take full ownership. Only by becoming ever more conscious of our spiritual nature can we move swiftly along the road to experiencing more and more bliss; and as we do, our relationships will mirror back to us that very depth, beauty, and joy.

You will be tested along the way to see what you believe, not in a judgmental or punitive way, but as a result of a higher intelligence guiding you and making sure your lessons stick. Tests can take many forms. Can you be happy in spite of being alone? Do you feel good about yourself even if your partner is not telling you great things to bolster your self-esteem? Might you lead an inspired life even if your partner is none too inspiring? There will be struggles to be sure, and things won't always look the way you wish they did. But once you recognize the power and grace that is always within and all around you, things will begin to get easier. And love will make itself known.

When we try to impose our will and manipulate love, it eludes us. The trick is to stop attempting to dominate the universe—and our relationships—and instead submit to the wisdom in our life right now, and to the fulfillment that *already resides* within us.

chapter four

Making the Shift

*Borrow the beloved's eyes. / Look through them and you'll see
the beloved's face . . .*

—RUMI, "CHECKMATE"

So now that you are aware of the obstacles, what do you do about them? It's easy to read about things, but it's another thing altogether to actually change their course. The tide cannot be turned through understanding alone. If you really want to know the bliss of soul mate love, you have to put into place a new way of thinking, behaving, and living. Only by changing the very nature of your response to life can you begin to enjoy the miraculous results this spiritual process promises. By engaging in a profound reworking of how you move through the world, you can usher in a level of love never before experienced. In a very real way, the level at which you operate determines the quality of character and depth of soul you draw to yourself; the partner you are with or the partner on the way is very much a reflection of what is inside you. As you change your energy, your relationship will transform; this is the challenge and the blessing of your life.

Breaking the Chain of Fear

As we saw earlier, messages about our self-worth and how to navigate the world are passed down through ripple effects from all the exchanges we and our family members have ever had. No relationship is insignificant, and everything contributes to the whole of who we are. We have inherited many patterns of thinking and behaving from our childhood experiences, but we have also picked up some new ones from the culture we live in. Regardless, it is up to us to see how and where we are bound by the chain of fear and then to break it.

At any given moment, we are constantly making decisions based on either love or fear. And we hardly think about them. For example, the decision to exercise can either arise out of "I'm going to exercise today because it makes me feel strong and it's good for my health," or "If I don't work out I will get fat and then no one will find me attractive." The same choice is driven by love on the one hand and by fear on the other. Although it sounds innocent enough to infuse a bit of cautionary thinking into our choices, if we are not careful we can easily slip into a habitually negative and fearful way of thinking. Once we are in fear mode, every move we make sets the stage for the next fearful thought. "Maybe my husband thinks I'm overweight; I wonder if he is still attracted to me. I'd better watch him for signs that he is straying." If we don't snap out of it, the train of fearful thoughts builds up such momentum that it's very difficult to stop.

For many of us, fear is a natural mindset. We might have learned from our parents that we'd better be on guard, or picked up their habit of worrying or being pessimistic. Or we listen to too much news that is geared toward the sensational so we believe the world is threatening or bad. In any case, if we continue to hook in to fear, we will continue to add links to the chain of negativity.

If we want to experience more love, we have to start making decisions based on love. We have to stop ourselves and ask, "Am I coming from fear or am I coming from love?"

But how do you just switch from one to the other, especially if you're confronting a lifetime of negative conditioning? Here are some suggestions for traversing the gulf between fear and love.

1. **Notice** when you are falling into fear mode (this includes being mean, judgmental, suspicious, punitive, etc.).

2. **Slow down** and take your time before saying or doing anything.

3. **Ask yourself what is coming up.** What is the monologue in your mind?

4. **Give yourself permission** to have your feelings.

5. **Make a decision** to shift into a more mature and loving place.

6. **Remind yourself that Spirit is always present** and that once your ego moves aside, Spirit will move through your life in a perfect and miraculous way.

Let's go through these steps so that you can draw on them when the opportunity next arises.

First of all, take **notice** when you are about to act in some less than loving way. Feel your body gearing up to respond angrily or judgmentally. Note how your jaw clenches or your stomach tightens or your heart races. Does your mind start building a case against your partner? Watch how quickly you gather evidence to bolster this attitude of aggression or victimization. You may be upset by something your partner did, or you might just be in a bad mood because you are hungry or tired. In this first step, practice being *mindful* of the fear response as it kicks into gear.

Next, just **slow down** and take a deep breath. This alone can break the cycle if you can actually hold off on acting based on what seems to be a natural impulse. When we are upset, we might do many things: yell, whine, retreat, call a friend to obsess, overeat, smoke, drink, or shut down and stop talking. I am not saying don't do those things, but before you do, take the time to be fully present. Often we say or do something we don't even intend because we just get caught up in the moment. If we can step back and take a few breaths, we might find ourselves more capable of dealing positively with the situation.

Third, **ask yourself what is coming up**. Often we substitute one emotion for another because we feel it's safer or more acceptable. For instance, if at first glance you think you are really angry, after you take a moment to think about it you might come to realize that beneath that anger lies fear. Since anger feels less vulnerable than fear or sadness, you might ride the anger wave without really connecting to what's going on below that. Or perhaps anger is the more genuine emotion lying beneath your sadness. If you were taught that anger was bad or impolite, you might have turned to depression as a way of keeping a lid on your growing rage. Getting to the bottom of our emotions is vital.

Next, **give yourself permission** to have your feelings,

whatever they may be. This does not mean it's okay to dump those feelings on your partner. Instead, sit with them in a safe environment and allow them to move through you. The more we try to control, get rid of, or stuff our feelings down, the more agitated we become. Also, if we don't own our feelings, we will most likely project them onto our partner and thus give up the power to do anything about them. Feelings are natural and necessary responses to life; they are an ever-changing part of us that adds texture and depth to our experience of life. We must listen to them but not stay attached to them. When you're going through a difficult time, remind yourself that whatever you are feeling now, you will not necessarily be feeling an hour or a week or a year from now. Things may be uncomfortable at the moment, but everything changes and shifts as long as you give it room to breathe. Surely it is important to communicate to your partner when they have affronted you in some way, but before doing that, try and separate out what is yours and what is theirs.

At this point, **make a decision** to switch gears so that anything you say or do is grounded in love. This doesn't mean you can't stand up for yourself; you can and should maintain clear boundaries. But you can deliver your communication in such a way that your partner feels the love behind it, along with your intention to get to the other side of this difficult moment. Ask yourself this: "How can I express myself in this situation in the most loving and most authentic way possible?" It isn't easy to pull yourself out of what feels like a righteous urge to criticize or blame or complain, but spiritual maturity doesn't come easily. It takes effort; it requires that we make a conscientious choice not to give way to our baser impulses.

And lastly, **remind yourself that Spirit is always present** and available to help us ascend to our higher nature. Once we relax our egos and surrender the situation to God, we can move aside and let that higher nature take its course. If we can see that everything that happens is just a backdrop for our spiritual development, we can stop taking things so personally and realize that everyone is just doing the best they can with what they have. Acknowledge your feelings and communicate them responsibly, then let go. Step away emotionally, allowing things to settle down and become clear; then let yourself be guided into living up to your potential.

By following these steps each and every time your fear gets engaged, you can profoundly change the way you relate to your partner (and everyone!), and by doing so you can alter the course of your life. Be a detective; find out where you could work harder to break yourself of old habits and patterns. Practice, practice, practice. And as you do, you will begin to knit together an entirely new and more joyful experience. As you move out of fear and into love, your partnership will also change, because when one person changes, they affect everyone and everything around them.

If we want to experience a transformation in the arena of relationship, we must start a revolution in our minds. We have to override our tendency to fall back on the negativity taught to us and lend our energy to a newer and kinder way of being.

Making Amends

As we learn to make a shift in ourselves and in our relationship, we become stronger, more loving, and more integrated people. In this process, we will likely come to realize that at various times in the past we have hurt our partners while caught in the throes of acting out of fear. Our actions have repercussions, and if we are to break through to a new level of relating, we must make amends to those we have affected in negative ways. To make amends is to take responsibility for causing pain and then make adjustments so we don't do it anymore. The word *amend* literally means "to fix."

It's challenging to muster up the courage to say we are sorry; it makes us feel vulnerable in a way that is extremely uncomfortable to the ego. As we consider how we have hurt our partner (or a past partner), we will undoubtedly notice ourselves going on the defensive. We'll tell ourselves we yelled because we felt unheard, teased because we felt rejected, or punished because we felt betrayed; there is always an excuse for being less than loving. Does "I wouldn't have charged up the credit card if only you had paid attention to me," or "If you weren't so mean to me I wouldn't have called you those names" sound familiar? It is our ego's nature to avoid culpability by justifying what we did, but that only keeps us stuck where we are. If we want to embrace our spiritual nature, we have to move past justifications.

It is one thing to acknowledge in the privacy of our own minds the extent of our unpleasant deeds, but the prospect of actually admitting them out loud to the person we hurt can overwhelm us with dread. "Why can't we just let sleeping dogs lie? Why aren't they making amends to me instead?" we might ask. Because it is *our* decision to work on ourselves, and therefore we are beholden to push ourselves toward whatever is required for Self-realization. We must confront the effect of our own actions and then build a bridge toward a more honorable and dignified relationship. We may not always be able to achieve total restitution, but we can at least take responsibility for our shortcomings and then do our best to win forgiveness.

It's important to note that it is best not to bring up details that would only hurt or serve to do further damage; this would be unnecessarily cruel. If admitting what we did would cause our partner to be upset at a cost to their safety or well-being, we would be better off quietly sending their soul an apology instead of unloading the whole story in an effort to clear our conscience. Lightening our own burden by transferring the weight to our partner is not making amends. There are no hard and fast rules as to what we should admit to and what we should withhold, so we have to think things through to be sure we're acting in everyone's best interest. And if some things are better left unsaid, it is essential that we acknowledge them to ourselves, to a trusted confidant, and to God. By sharing our admissions out loud, we deepen our insight into what needs to be worked on in our character.

There are small violations and large ones; each is important to address. While some might have rolled off our partner's back, others might have triggered depression or rage. And although they may not wish to talk about it, chances are the wounds persist beneath their conscious awareness. Each unkindness has the potential to affect that person's life for the worse. It is not ours to decide how and when someone should "get over it," but to make it easier to arrive at forgiveness and healing.

What kind of injury requires making amends? Whenever we have caused mental, emotional, or physical pain by acting lovelessly, we are responsible for making amends. Our actions might have been overt or passive-aggressive, but their effect is unmistakable. Any time we intend to cause hurt, we lose our spiritual momentum. If by our attempt to dominate a stressful situation we have handled things poorly, amends are called for.

At this point it might be helpful to identify the times you have acted in hurtful ways toward your partner. You can apply this exercise to past partners also because the more we clean up the messes we have made, the brighter our energy can shine. Try and detail each event, noting what kicked off the behavior and the extent of the harm it caused. Here is an example.

When Amends Are Called For

November 24: I called attention to my wife's exaggeration of how hard she worked on the Thanksgiving dinner. She was going on and on about all the things she did to make the day perfect, when I knew she had bought some of the dishes from a local restaurant. She has always prided herself on being a wiz in the kitchen and was extremely embarrassed when I chided her in front of a dozen of our friends. She was trying to impress them and I completely deflated her. When I think about why I did it, my first excuse is that it was her fault for lying in the first place. But upon further investiga-

tion, I realized I took a jab at her because I'd been feeling neglected and unloved. I owe her an apology as well as a vow to be more responsible and mature with my communications in the future. She tries very hard to make a beautiful event of the holidays and she deserves better from me.

It's important to see how you acted inappropriately, but it's even more vital that you understand what was driving you. Once you can identify and sit with the underlying feelings that motivated your actions, you can address what needs to be tended to in your own psyche. Also, by discussing these deeper feelings with your partner in conjunction with the apology, you create an opening for your partner to know and relate to you better. Of course, admitting to something in and of itself will not be enough; you will need to find a way to convey your commitment to do better in a direct and unmistakable manner. A promise to undertake therapy or work in a spiritual program may help assure your partner that you are committed to changing your behavior. Be willing to be accountable and be patient in regaining the trust.

When making amends, we should consider our timing as well as our approach. It would be wise to wait for a moment when things are calm and there is time to devote to the conversation. We need to be as tactful and objective as possible. There is no need to rehash events for the purpose of encouraging our partners to share in the culpability; this is about moving through *our* stuff, not theirs. We shouldn't expect a return apology or even instant forgiveness from our partner; they will have their own sense of things. Once we express ourselves in a genuine way and with good intentions, we have to step back and allow our partner to digest what was discussed.

Here is an example of what making amends might sound like.

Making Amends

I want to apologize to you for embarrassing you so publicly about not cooking all the dishes on Thanksgiving. I can tell I really hurt your feelings and made our guests feel uncomfortable. Not as an excuse, but by way of background, I think I was feeling insecure because everyone was praising you and telling you how great you made the day. No one acknowledged that I had anything to do with the festivities and I started feeling underappreciated. I was feeling sorry for myself and I acted out inappropriately. I am noticing that I get into these funks when I don't get what I think is enough attention at any given time. This emotion is clearly coming from somewhere deep in my past, which makes me realize I have some work to do on myself. I really am sorry for my rude and thoughtless comments. I know how hard you worked and instead of being grateful, I dishonored you in front of people. I was wrong and I feel terrible about it. To help make sure it doesn't happen again, I have signed up for a course in how to work through childhood wounds. I hope you can find it in your heart to forgive me.

A good apology is well thought out, heartfelt, and solution oriented. With some practice, making amends becomes easier. If we start small, we can build confidence by seeing how significantly the relationship benefits from even these attempts.

That said, there are no guarantees of success when we make amends. Our partners may not give us their approval and forgiveness; we might feel sorry that we even brought things up. But that is the chance we take to clear the air. The more sincere and authentic we are in our request for forgiveness, the more likely our partner will be to let go and move on. At worst, we can expect another flare-up of the same old sentiments that got us into trouble in the first place. At best, we might get a warm embrace and a pledge to move on in more mutually supportive ways. Either way, we need to keep checking in with our intentions to be sure we're staying on track. All we can do is work our side of the fence and leave the rest to our partner and to Spirit.

After we have made amends, we need not dwell in re-
morse. If we truly feel sorry for how we have acted, we
won't do it again. Making amends should be daunting
enough to keep us on the straight and narrow, but the
acid test will be the conflict just over the horizon.

Forgiveness

At this point, you have hopefully been able to admit
where you were wrong and made a commitment to
change the behavior . But how do you let go of wrongdo-
ing that was directed toward you? As important as it is to
request forgiveness, it is equally crucial to grant it—
whether or not someone asks you to do so. Just as unresolved guilt will block the flow of goodwill and fulfillment,
resentment will stand in the way of experiencing deep and
soulful love.

We create untold suffering for ourselves by holding on
to grievances and grudges. We grind our teeth, toss and
turn in fitful nights of sleep, and give ourselves agita by
mulling over how we were mistreated and what should
have happened instead. Or we may just close our hearts.
But if you think about it, none of this changes what happened, and in fact, it only serves to keep us attached to
the event that hurt us. As much as we were distressed at
the time, the real suffering comes from our prolonged and
unresolved response to it.

We may nag, pout, brood, or issue ultimatums, but we cannot get someone to "make things better" for us. We can't make them be what we want them to be. We can't control the behavior of our partners, nor can we instill in them our values system. The only thing we *can* do is work on ourselves. We can weigh our feelings, communicate our displeasure in a responsible way, and then ask for spiritual assistance in letting go. Let's look at each of these three steps individually.

First, we have to acknowledge and allow our feelings, because if we don't, they will pop up as ill health or inappropriate behavior later on. When we feel attacked or hurt, we not only process it intellectually, but we also feel it bodily; it may give us a backache, or we might experience it as a cramped stomach. Some of us literally feel pain in our hearts when a loved one hurts us, and others feel like they can't breathe. By noticing how feelings manifest in our body, we can remain alert and keep the channels open within us and within our relationship.

If you are angry, a great way to move the energy is to scream out loud (alone and in a very private place) or hit a pillow or a punching bag. In many cases, anger is a perfectly valid thing to feel, but holding on to it isn't healthy. I find that once you can "physicalize" what is going on inside, you become more clear about what the next step should be. If sadness arises, let yourself cry. Wail. Let the tears connect you to your center and set free whatever needs to be released.

Sometimes your emotions may be frighteningly strong and other times they will pass through you with hardly a sign. Let them be whatever they are; don't push and don't repress. The wisdom of releasing feelings is that it will free you from old patterns of thinking and behaving; you will no longer get caught up in the old attack/defend cycle and you will move more quickly through difficult situations.

The next step in getting to forgiveness is to communicate your displeasure or pain calmly and evenly. You need not present yourself as a victim, but as a dignified adult with healthy boundaries. Often, your partner won't even know what they did wrong; they might have been on automatic pilot and you were an innocent bystander to their acting out. By letting them know what they did and how it affected you, you will release yourself from the burden of carrying around unfinished business.

The conversation might sound something like this: "You know, Susan, by taking that two-hour lunch with your old boyfriend, I feel like you disregarded your commitment to me. It seems inappropriate that you would spend so much time alone together, and I really don't feel comfortable with it. Not only do I feel hurt and angry, but I am embarrassed just thinking about what other people might assume. If, in the future, you want to get together with him, will you please discuss it with me first?" No drama, just simple, heartfelt communication.

Lastly, we can ask for spiritual assistance in letting go and moving forward. Sometimes it's hard to get past things; we are human. But if we resolve what we can through acknowledging, feeling, and communicating, we can leave the rest to Spirit. We can set our intention to forgive, and then ask God to give us the strength and peace of mind to see it through. If we have a genuine desire to heal and move forward, we can surrender to Spirit those last traces of resentment that we can't seem to shake, trusting that everything will be handled in a divine manner. We can say, *"God, take this pain from me and help me to heal. Help me to know that this is not personal and that he did the best he could at the time. I admit I am still full of rage, and I don't really wish the best for him. Not yet. But I am willing to see things differently and ask for your assistance in getting there. Please guide us both into being our best potential. Amen."*

Of course, there are things we can forgive but shouldn't necessarily forget. If someone has done us real harm, or places us in emotional, spiritual, or physical danger, we need to take stock, evaluate their pattern of behavior, and realistically assess its prospects of changing. We can forgive at a time when it's safe to do so, and we can make peace from a distance. Forgiving someone after they have cheated on you repeatedly, for instance, is important in keeping your heart open. But it would not be wise to keep investing your trust in that person. Or if you have been physically abused, you can set your intention to forgive while still getting yourself out of harm's way. Forgiving someone certainly doesn't mean you should expose yourself to future harm.

We cannot know how another person arrived at their current disposition. We are all learning to be better, trying hard to overcome lower instincts, and we will get there when we get there. We each have our challenges and we have all made missteps. If we assume that our partners are doing their best given what their soul has encountered, perhaps we can find peace in knowing that any hurt they have inflicted is more about them than it is about us. Malevolent behavior is just an extension or expression of self-hatred. When our partner acts in loveless ways, it means they are feeling loveless inside; they are in pain and so they project pain. It is not our job to absorb their distress or fix their problems, but we can be aware of their suffering and not allow it to stick to us. By not taking their remarks or gestures to heart, we can leave them with the full weight of what they attempted to place on us. The true meaning of forgiveness is in allowing someone the space to find their way. If we are to see things as they really are, we will know that ultimately we are all innocent and perfect because God created us that way. Everything else is just an illusion of the ego. Here is another prayer I use when I am tempted to hold onto blame.

Prayer for Forgiveness

God, may I see my partner for the innocent that he really is. May the hurt he has caused be wiped away by my awareness of how he suffers inside. I am willing to release the story of who did what to whom. It doesn't matter; all that matters is that I keep my heart open and available to love. I release my partner, and with him his deeds, comments, and gestures. He did not know how to do things differently, but I know. And I forgive him. May we both move forward in a way that is best for both of us. May I be lifted into peace and serenity, and may we all be liberated from the bondage of fear. Amen.

We can forgive without being self-righteous; we can consent to allow each other's humanity. None of us are perfect if we look through the limited eyes of the ego; but the deeper we look, the more clearly we will see the spark of Spirit trying to catch flame.

chapter five

The Way of Love

*It is as if a raindrop fell from heaven into a stream or foun-
tain and became one with the water in it so that never again
can the raindrop be separated from the water of the stream; or
as if a little brook ran into the sea and there was thencefor-
ward no means of distinguishing its water from the ocean; or
as if a brilliant light came into a room through two windows
and though it comes in divided between them, it forms a single light inside.*

—St. Teresa of Avila, quoted in
The Virago Book of Spirituality, Edited by Sarah Anderson

The purpose of any relationship is to
provide an arena for growth, inspiring us to value and
nurture our interdependence with one another. As we
learn to be with someone in this way, we discover a richer
form of love, one which is undeniably the next phase of a
soulful relationship. This is not only about what we can
do, but who we can *be*. As we clarify and deepen our role
as loving partner, we move from the intense work of re-
moving the glitches of our character to learning how to
relate on a daily basis. Here are some important ways to

create the space for Spirit to move and express through a relationship.

Commitment

Committing yourself to a relationship means more than promising not to see anyone else; it means you consider your partner's welfare as seriously as you do your own. You are saying "I promise to be loving, and I will support your growth in every way I can." This means that when the going gets tough, you don't cut and run; you hang in there and work things through. And when things are great, you celebrate and enjoy the ride together.

If we want a soulful relationship, we need to nurture it by *honoring the Spirit* within our partner. In Hindu cultures, a common greeting is *Namaste*, which means "the Divine within me salutes the Divine within you"; how wonderful it would be if we could all regard each other in this way. By approaching a relationship with honor and respect, we treat it as if it were holy. And so it is. If God were looking at you through the eyes of your partner, wouldn't you have more patience, give more support, and make whatever efforts necessary? Wouldn't you be your very kindest and most loving self? Of course you would, and you would trust that whatever was going on between you was a backdrop that only served to fine-tune your spiritual maturity. You would see that the juice of life is in how we interact with each other, how steadily we can hold to love rather than bow to fear.

So your promise of commitment is really to maintain an open heart as you work things through. Say you want to start a family, for instance, but your partner doesn't. Your commitment to him is not demonstrated by forgoing your dream for children, but rather by expressing your desire in a strong, loving way. Conventional commitment might sound like, "I really want to have a baby but I don't want to lose you, so I will give up my dream and do what you want." This approach is likely to sow the seeds of resentment. A spiritually based commitment might sound more like, "I really want to have a baby, and I can see that this is not something you are ready for. Can we revisit this conversation in six months when you might be more open to it? If not, and you are really sure it's a closed issue, perhaps we should consider what route we can take so both of us will be happy. I love you, and I know you love me, so let's find a way to do what is best for both of us." See the difference? The old way of viewing commitment is laced with fear, while a spiritually minded commitment is imbued with love and an underlying intention to have the best outcome for both parties. It says, "I commit to you while at the same time I understand that we might have different ideas and goals."

As nice as it would be to have both partners equally committed to the same things, it is almost always the case that one person will be more invested in something than the other. Priorities will shift and change between you at various points along the way, but one thing you can always count on, and control, is your own level of integrity.

Commitment requires discipline, to be sure. The word *discipline* derives from the Latin word discipulus, which means "pupil" or "follower of a teacher." To be disciplined, then, is to attempt to do what a teacher would do. Every spiritual tradition instructs us to love rather than fear, forgive rather than condemn, and to cooperate rather than demand. Discipline comes from following those teachings and applying them to all our relationships, romantic and otherwise. We need to constantly remind ourselves to check our internal compass to ensure we are on track.

To make a commitment also means setting your intention. By doing so, you clarify for yourself—and the powers that be—what you want for the relationship. That clarity draws to you circumstances that reflect your goal, and, maddeningly, also attracts whatever stands in the way of your having that goal. This means that as soon as you make a commitment to someone or something new, you can be pretty sure that anything that runs counter to that commitment will materialize in an effort to keep you in your old comfort zone. For instance, if I make a new commitment to being a vegetarian, I might soon find myself in a situation where I'm really hungry and all that is being served are hamburgers and chicken fingers. I might see articles championing a meat-based high protein diet in every magazine I thumb through, and my old-school doctor might even warn me about the perils of not getting enough protein. Supported by ego, my old self—the part of me I am trying to evolve out of—is showing up to test my resolve. "Are you sure you really mean this? Can I tempt you to change your mind?" But these questions are good; they serve the purpose of making sure I am clear about my intention and have the conviction to hold to it. It is also a way of making me face all my fears and doubts so that as I advance on this new path, I can feel confident because I will have addressed my trepidations. In much the same way, when we consider committing to someone at a new level, all our fears—hidden or overt—come forth so that we can deal with them, make the desired shift, and then move forward. The Dark Voice will inevitably have a few things to say as you move toward a more enlightened way of being. Don't cut it off. Listen, and then keep sticking to your spiritual principles.

We can't dictate what the details of a relationship should look like; our moods and desires and situations are always changing. We can't say, for instance, "I will continue to love and honor you . . . so long as you are in a cheerful mood and want to live in Los Angeles and you don't get fired from your job and agree to have three children." That is not a commitment; it's holding someone hostage to your dream. A spiritually based commitment sounds more like, "I am committed to you when you are happy and I'm with you when you are sad. I really want to live in Los Angeles, but I understand it may not feel right to you, so perhaps we could look at other cities with warm climates. And I know you are worried about losing your job, but if you are fired, we will work things out and I will be with you as you figure out your next move." Real commitment means approaching your partner with respect and treating him or her lovingly. This doesn't mean you aren't allowed to have frustrated feelings and it doesn't even mean you can't decide to part ways at some point if you both see that what you want out of life is entirely different. It only means you keep giving the best of yourself in accordance with your spiritual principles. Spiritual principles always point us toward joy, freedom, and interdependence, and so if we are vigilant about keeping our intentions pure, we can navigate all the twists and turns that life will surely present to us.

Let's take a look at where your commitment lies now.

Where I Stand

1. My overall spiritual intention is _____

_____.

2. In my relationship, I intend to demonstrate

   _____ .

3. I can do this by _____ .
4. When the fear and doubt arises to challenge
   me, I will deal with it by _____ .
5. The hurdle I must overcome is _____

   _____ .

6. My commitment to my partner is _____

   _____ .

7. My commitment to the relationship is ____

   _____ .

This exercise will help you to formulate and refine your intentions; it will assist you in unraveling all your conflicting thoughts and emotions so that you can see what choices you are making. By clarifying things for yourself you can more readily redirect the energy in the relationship toward love and integrity. The central theme of any conscious intention or commitment should always be to move toward wholeness by regarding your partner as an extension of God. And of course, he or she is exactly that. Your job is to set the stage for an enlightened partnership by continuing to remove the obstacles to love. Choose to see your partner's innocence, and that innocence will become more evident. This is a path of soulful love, a curriculum for learning to embrace a higher way of being. It takes practice, but if you keep putting one foot in front of the other, your commitment will guide you to love at its most glorious.

Communication

We want more out of partnership than beautiful wedding pictures; we want dynamism, shared vision, and growing insight into the meaning of life. We seek that kind of synergy instinctively, and we can nurture it with effective communication. Through *purposeful interaction* we weave the connective fiber of a soulful and successful relationship. As individuals we can only go so far in pushing through boundaries of self, but with our soul mate we can take a quantum leap towards Oneness.

Falling in love is largely a result of chemistry; we are attracted to a person by forces outside the realm of our conscious awareness. We meet our partners and, depending on how things work out, we may commit to them. But what *sustains* the magic is not white-knuckle determination to stay together through thick and thin, but how effectively we *relate* to each other.

The backbone of a successful partnership lies in how adept it is at handling whatever life throws its way. By establishing a *conscientious rapport*, we can thrive in any circumstance. The following four-point strategy can help us do so.

What to Keep in Mind as We Communicate

1. Courtesy
2. Responsibility
3. Honest and assertive expression
4. Flow

To begin with, we need to give each other the **courtesy** of being able to speak without interruption or judgment. We can hear what our partner has to say and then respond so they know they've been heard. Slow down and listen. Being heard clearly is not to be underestimated, since so many arguments stem from the frustration of not being able to get a point across. So when your partner says, "I'm too tired to have sex; can we do it tomorrow?" you can mirror back with, "Oh, wow, I didn't realize you were so tired; you must have had a really tough day. Tell me what's going on." In this way you are acknowledging what they say rather than skipping over it and going straight to your frustration by responding with, "Whatever. There never seems to be time for me." The first response builds a bridge while the second creates separation. If we can have patience and really listen, the stage will be set for healthy discourse and resolution.

We can also take **responsibility** for our feelings, which means not blaming our partner for "making" us feel anything. "You make me nuts when you leave your clothes all over the place" gives way to "When you leave your clothes all over the place I feel overwhelmed and angry because I already have so much to do." Then a simple suggestion for making the situation more workable, such as "Let's hire someone to come in and clean once a week," can move you out of the problem and into a solution.

Still another essential element of healthy communication is **honest and assertive expression** of what we think, need, and want. We can't expect our partners to guess when and where we could use help or anticipate what will assuage our pain. Being indirect or cagey will only produce confusion and misunderstanding. Instead we can learn to present our opinions, desires, and needs directly, keeping manipulation to a minimum. "I would so love it if you acknowledged from time to time how hard I work to help provide this lifestyle we enjoy; it means a lot to me to know that you are happy, and I feel buoyed when you let me know that I am contributing in positive ways." This is far more effective than growing ever more resentful at working hard and never getting the acknowledgement you're looking for. Or, if you are upset at feeling disregarded, you could present your case calmly and evenly by saying, "I'd like to talk about something with you. When you ignore my questions, I feel like I have to push all the harder to get your attention. I'm left with the feeling that you don't care about my situation, and I get angry about it. It would really be great if we could take some time to discuss this." If something is important to you, speak up.

And most importantly, we need to be able to **flow** with whatever happens. Life and relationships go so much more easily when we can take things as they come. Things have a way of working themselves out if you can just make room for that to happen. What seems insurmountable today may look very different a week from now—or even after a nap or a short meditation. By *resisting* what comes up, we add weight to our problems. If, for instance, your partner is in a cranky mood and seems not to want to talk, don't push it. Assume they are going through whatever they need to go through; if they are going to snap out of it, the impetus is most likely going to be provided by them, not you. You could just offer, "I can see that you need some space. I'm just letting you know I'm here if you want to talk. If not, that is perfectly okay. I might go out to the movies, or read my book, but I will still be available to you if you need me."

We can roll with each other's moods without getting drawn into them; we don't have to solve them either. Moodiness and trying times are all part of life, all part of what ultimately serves to make us stronger, deeper people. If we keep the lines of communication open while still giving each other space, we can move through things with a fair amount of ease.

Communication is more than just talking. We read each other by tone of voice, gesture, and other body language. Tightly controlled movements while cooking dinner or pursed lips at mealtime may be your way of communicating dissatisfaction and irritation, but your partner may have no idea what is going on. Or they may be afraid to ask for fear of triggering an explosion. You might hope you can get your point across indirectly, but really the likelihood of misunderstanding shoots up exponentially. On the other hand, when you drop what you are doing and sit down to speak with your partner, you send a clear message: "Our relationship is a priority. I believe we can find common ground if we work on this."

We often convey how much (or how little) we care in ways we may not even consciously choose. You send a message of "I don't really care about you" when you open the newspaper while your partner is talking. A slight turn away when your partner reaches for you speaks volumes, as does a smile in your eyes when they relate the day's events. You can tell when someone is being open, warm, and receptive, and you can tell when love is being withheld no matter what the words are. It's up to us to become more aware of ourselves so that we can be more responsible with the energy we put out.

Again, it's not just what we say, but how we say it, that sends a message. You could choose to say to your partner, "I am not spending any more weekends at your parents' house. I understand you will be angry, but I have had enough. You can go by yourself if you want to." If you do, your partner might well feel backed into a corner. Even though you are stating your case clearly and without drama, it leaves them little room to maneuver. The subtext is, "I am thinking only of myself and I don't care what you want. You can take it or leave it." You would do far better if you said something to the effect of, "Honey, I am getting wound up about leaving for your parents' house on Friday, and it's only Tuesday. How do you feel about going there? I know how much you love seeing them, but I find myself running out of things to talk about. What are your thoughts? Help me figure this out so we can both enjoy the weekend as much as possible." In this way, you are opening the subject for discussion; you are stating your case while at the same time respecting your partner's needs so that they won't have to go on the defensive.

To clarify once more, it's not about saying things in just the right way (although that is surely helpful). It is more intuitive than that. It's about getting in touch with how you feel and sharing it in a way that honors your partner and leaves room for them to share their feelings with you.

What we really want to say—the message that actually comes across—can be detected more in the *subtext* than in the words themselves. You may smile and say, "Have a nice day, dear," but it reads as "Drop dead!" if what you are feeling deep down inside is rage. If we aren't in touch with what lies beneath the surface, how can our partner possibly respond in a way that makes a real connection? Our work is to *know ourselves* to the best of our ability and be as clear as possible in our communication. Underlying any communication should be the intention to connect rather than separate.

From time to time, many of us are guilty of being passive-aggressive. We might find ourselves not liking something our partner is doing, but not knowing how to address it without risking an argument. So we use words that can't be held against us but still convey our desire to criticize. If Hank says to Sue with a certain hostile tone in his voice, "Boy, do you have the life," the words themselves are innocent enough, but she will likely hear the underlying criticism. If Hank isn't aware of his real feelings, or doesn't want to be clear about them, they could get into muddy waters. But instead of defending the "good life" Hank seems to resent (maybe she regularly lunches with her girlfriends or spends money on getting her hair and nails done), Sue could nip things in the bud by saying, "Hank, what would you like me to take away from that comment? Are you feeling angry that I am enjoying my life? If so, let's talk about it. I'd really like to know what you mean." If you approach the matter with the intent of *connecting* rather than sparring or polarizing, the passive aggression just won't stand up. Things may come up that are uncomfortable, and a confrontation might even ensue, but at least everything will be on the table so a real solution can be worked out. The more clearly we express ourselves, the more authentically our partners will respond to us.

As we remain open and responsive to the complete range of our own feelings as well as those of our partner, the more alive the relationship will be. When we allow for the complete array of human experiences to come up and move through us, we become more and more intimate with each other. Remember, we are meant to *deal* with our stuff. If we are to evolve spiritually, we have to support each other in opening up to our deeper feelings.

Sex

Sex is one of the great mysteries of life. We crave it, we are in awe of it, and more often than not it drives us to our limits and beyond. It is a force completely out of our conscious control. Is it the song of Spirit? Or is it the Dark Voice calling us into misbegotten or secreted impulses? Either way, sex is an unquestionably compelling force pushing us along the path to knowing ourselves better.

Passion is a clear sign that what you feel for someone is soulful. Physical attraction speaks through the body in a way that is unmistakable. It literally pulls you toward a person or situation as if your body was in league with a higher power trying to grab your attention. You can tell something big is going on, and you are driven to find out what it is. Sexual energy trumps reason no matter how hard you try to introduce your better judgment; you simply can't deny what is happening in your body. It can grab your attention to the point of obsession and make a tidy life come loose at the seams.

The tug of sexual attraction is to be explored (if not by acting out, then through imagination) and learned from. What and who turns us on is as revealing as what repels us, and sometimes the two go hand in hand. It is as if the truth of who we are wants to be revealed in all its naked glory. As beautiful and joyous as sex often is, it can also be dark. The soul knows all our hidden complexities and works to bring them to light. And the more conscious we are about what lies beneath our impulses, the more adept we can become at being awake and conscious in our relationship.

Because interpersonal chemistry remains beyond our control, it serves as an excellent reminder that we are not pulling all the strings. We can't *will* attraction, nor can we snuff it out. It comes in its own time and place and usually bowls us over with its force. This is not to say that the person you are attracted to is necessarily a great partner for you, but they get your attention for a reason. To embrace sexuality for what it can teach us, we have to look at *why* we are attracted to someone; what is it about them that hooks us?

If you think you have found the One because your body lights up when thinking of someone, you may indeed have found a lifelong partner, but you could also have been drawn to that person for a specific healing your soul requires. If, for instance, you are overwhelmingly attracted to Mr. Tall, Dark, and Handsome, but after a month of dating it turns out he is abusive, you may question what the chemistry was all about. You are still undeniably drawn to him, but you are no longer in fantasy land; clearly this guy has some issues, and you wonder why you can't turn away from someone who is so hurtful.

Instead of berating yourself for not leaving him, you could look at the situation more closely. What feels familiar about it? What aspect of your psyche is trying to be healed? What part of you wants to engage with that kind of behavior, and why? Perhaps someone in early childhood was abusive and your soul is ready to heal the damage they wrought. Maybe it's time for you to work out that you are worthwhile and wonderful despite the message that the malevolent person conveyed to you. Perhaps the only way you can come to terms with the fact that you're okay is to face the demons that only another abusive person reawakens in you. The soul doesn't let sleeping dogs lie.

You might have gone out with Mr. Tall, Dark, and Handsome because you were attracted to him, but your soul was stirred in his presence *because he offered a very specific healing.* Once you explore what the attraction has drawn you into—perhaps some unresolved or unreleased emotion—you can attend to it. In this way, you become freed of old burdens that weighed down on your soul. You will then no longer need to repeat the painful dynamic. The attraction will have done its work if you stay observant and take in its lesson.

When I went through such a situation myself, I tried desperately to figure out what I needed to learn so I could move on from my destructive relationship. I knew I had to leave, but the attraction was such that I just couldn't seem to break away despite my friends' and family's urging. In hindsight, though, staying was the best thing I could have done, because the pain of being with someone who was cruel and untrustworthy forced me to look inside myself to see what was responding to this man's energy. Clearly I wouldn't have stayed with him if what he was doing didn't resonate somehow with what I felt I deserved. Something was trying to be healed in me and finally I began to pay attention.

By looking squarely at what was coming up for me, I could at last confront and let go of a long-held belief that I was unworthy. Peter (the name I will call him) reflected back to me my own self-hatred in ways I could no longer ignore. Even the sex had been disturbingly cold. But I had invited him into my life. I had wanted him in the worst way, and no one could talk me out of it.

The dramas that ensued over the next few years were staggering, yet somehow I knew we were meant to engage in this dance. There were things I needed to learn. Peter crushed me, but he didn't kill me. What he destroyed was my old self, and my old ideas of who I was and what my limitations were. No amount of "improving" myself had won him over. I finally realized that it didn't matter if I had the brains of Albert Einstein, performed like the Cirque du Soleil in bed, or looked like a supermodel (not that I was any of this); I would never be "enough" to win Peter's love. He continued to cheat on me and to be abusive no matter what I did to try to make him happy. Peter was dealing with his own "hungry ghost," and I was just spinning my wheels and exhausting myself by trying to please him.

Finally, after I was humiliated one time too many, it dawned on me that my self-worth could not and should not be contingent on someone else's approval. I had to finally realize that who I am has nothing to do with another person's perception. I am worthwhile for the simple reason that I am alive and doing the best I can. God created me, just like everyone else, to be perfect and happy; and with that realization, I began to shed some very old and damaged self-perceptions. This was a huge awakening for me, since I spent my entire adult life believing that if I wanted happiness, if I wanted to feel love, I had to twist myself into a pretzel to get it. This was a thicket of beliefs that I needed to confront on my spiritual path, and Peter was an excellent catalyst for me to see it clearly once and for all.

After reading a lot of self-help books, going to spiritual meetings, and taking courses to better understand myself, I came to find serenity and empowerment in knowing that I—like everyone—am made up of Spirit, and that my well-being depends on embracing that inner truth rather than allowing someone else to determine whether or not I am "good enough." If I wanted self-esteem, I realized I would have to find and build it from within. By being with Peter, I went through a very dark and difficult time, but in the end, I was spurred to see that my beliefs had strayed too far from my spiritual center.

As I began to digest this new awareness and to rely more on prayer, meditation, and building my self-esteem (I started doing volunteer work, exercised regularly, and got my financial life together), my emotional and sexual connection to Peter fizzled. As the lesson my soul was guiding me to was now learned, the chemistry that compelled my attention was no longer present. It certainly wasn't clear in the beginning of our relationship, but the physical attraction I felt for Peter brought me a crucial lesson.

The only way to find out what a so-called negative attraction holds for you is to pay attention to it. Watch and
listen to what comes up within your mind and in your
heart. Observe what wants to be expressed in and through
you. Does the attraction bring up your insecurity, for instance? If so, perhaps it is your insecurity you need to look
at and begin to heal. Or perhaps it brings up your urge to
caretake, to fix. Whatever it is, observe what energies
within you need to be loosed, processed, and harmonized.
Notice how the physical attraction resonates with what
your soul longs to bring into balance, and then see if the
attraction still has its power once you tend to those energies. I suggest that as you make peace with what is discovered, your core beliefs will shift and change, *as will
your attractions*.

On the sunnier side of attraction, Spirit also resides in
the joyful aspects of romantic love. You can physically experience Spirit in every cell of your being when you meet
someone with whom you share chemistry. You offer and
share yourself, and it feels so good, and so right. When we
experience sexual abandon, are we not stepping beyond
the boundaries of ego and becoming one with each other?
In the sweetest way we are being reminded of our true
interconnectedness, our Oneness.

Passion shakes us into revelation by commanding us
to tend to the soul's urgings. Sometimes we forget who
we are until we are awakened by the chemistry of a new

or renewed relationship. Then we recall our nurturing side, or our wild side, or our adventurous side. Passion wakes us up and pushes us beyond what we thought our limits were. We feel more in touch with life, more creative. Suddenly everything seems possible as passion works at every level to expand our awareness.

Just as we can get hooked on the destructive side of passion, though, we can also become addicted to the rush of getting physically intimate with someone. Such closeness can make us feel great, but if we start counting on it to always make us feel good, we can get in trouble. When we look to sex to fulfill our every need or to express emotions that aren't comfortable, obsession and compulsion arise. Sex is not to be used to medicate or exploit our feelings, nor is it to replace a comprehensive spiritual path. Sex is not God, and we would do well to maintain our spiritual practice so that the powerful lure of passion doesn't blind us to our deeper path. It is illuminating and healthy to come to know and understand the sexual aspect of ourselves, but we need to maintain balance in the other areas of our life as well. Fantasies and lust are fun, but they are not to overtake us.

I want to mention here that the notion of acting out fantasies with a partner does not apply to psychopathology, which is a whole other matter. Rape, pedophilia, and other sexual crimes are clearly cases that should not be freely explored. As with all "sins", these acts are demonstrative of where a person has missed the mark and gone wildly astray. If such a person sincerely wishes to get back on a path of light, I believe it is possible. Because addiction and perversion are deeply embedded (and possibly genetic) codes of behavior, it is helpful to remember the ancestral chain of which we are a part. Some people are just born with a gene that leads them to act out in harmful ways; others were wounded in early childhood in ways that carved a groove for sexual deviation to keep playing itself out. But in any case, it is the personality—the lower self—that is guilty, but the soul—the greater Self—wants to heal and recall its innocence.

Shifting the tide requires enormous commitment on the part of the criminal or addict; they have to want a change and be willing to undergo intensive and often painful work. I recommend getting help from all angles: emotional (specialized and multipronged therapy), physical (appropriate drugs, if necessary, as prescribed by a doctor), and spiritual (twelve-step approach such as Sex Addicts Anonymous). Even in this, the most shameful dungeon of humanity, compassion is called for. Although they must be held accountable for their actions, these people are in spiritual bondage and they could use our prayers. Enough said; I just want to be sure there is no confusion between criminal activity and healthy exploration of sexuality.

Passion often leads us into forbidden or forgotten corners of the psyche. Our fantasies can certainly show us where we might be stuck in an old groove or longing to express some submerged part of ourselves. We can note by our fantasies where we might be out of balance and need to integrate different aspects of our personalities energetically. Remember, we are yin and yang, feminine and masculine, but if we get out of balance, one or the other energy can take hold and demand equalization. A man who is fierce and bullish in business (out-of-balance masculine) may have fantasies of being forcefully dominated (out-of-balance feminine) in the bedroom. Being extreme in our outer world often causes an equal and opposite extreme in our inner world; our fantasy life is one area which illustrates how we might need to strike a balance and create harmony. Once we accept ourselves and come to understand why certain things turn us on, we will come to know and love ourselves—and each other—more.

I once had a client, Joe, who came to me because he was disturbed by how his sexual life was playing out. As much as he wanted to be "a normal guy" in the bedroom, the only thing that seemed to turn him on was to be dominated and humiliated by his wife. Until she tied him up, beat him with a hairbrush, and taunted him about being "girly," he couldn't get excited, and he wasn't able to climax until he felt firmly and completely under her control. Joe didn't like to think of himself this way, and he shuddered as he told me about his sexual proclivities. But as much as Joe tried to get turned on in other ways, nothing seemed to work.

I asked Joe to describe what he was like otherwise, how he presented himself in his everyday life. He went on to tell me, with a little smirk of pride, how he ran a successful business and was known to be unrelenting with his workers. He didn't believe that anything could be done thoroughly or well if he didn't ride his workers hard.

I asked him if he thought this forcefulness might be a bit extreme. After fiercely defending having to be a tough guy, it slowly began to dawn on him that he was tired of trying to force things to work out. In fact, he was afraid that all his success would slip away completely if he loosened his grip for even a minute. He saw that he came from a long line of tough guys, and that it was the only way he knew how to be. In a moment of profound realization, Joe saw that his sexual desire to be put down, beaten, and controlled was the polar opposite of how he navigated the rest of his life. His desire served as an *indicator* that, when analyzed, showed him that he needed to create balance, and find the middle ground. He saw that the way he conducted business was too domineering, and his sexuality was just the other side of the same coin.

I advised Joe to take some small steps toward being less macho and more supportive to the people who worked for him. If he could approach his work with a bit more feminine energy (kindness, support, surrender), he would be less inclined to act out his suppressed femininity in the bedroom.

Sure enough, once Joe began to let go of his tight hold at work, his sexual urges also shifted. He became a more balanced man in his life and lost the desire to act out extreme desires in the bedroom. I am not positing that Joe's fantasy was wrong or that acting it out was bad, but because Joe was uncomfortable with it, we looked closely at what those urges might have been trying to show him. It wasn't easy work for him to do, but Joe was committed to moving forward in his development as a human being and wanted a healthy and mutually respectful relationship with his wife. As he came to better understand his inner workings, many aspects of his life shifted.

Our fantasies can show us where we might be stuck psychically or long to express some hidden part of ourselves. They provide clues about where we need to strike a balance and create harmony. Once we accept ourselves and come to understand why certain things turn us on, we will cease acting out unconsciously and move into sexual maturity. Self-knowledge and self-love are the foundation of spiritual growth. Only by looking squarely and nonjudgmentally at that which stirs us can we stay the course of reintegrating all aspects of ourselves into healthy wholeness.

Of course, any time we seek to act out a fantasy, we need to honor our partner's safety and well-being as well as our own. If acting out a fantasy would hurt someone, we should consider carefully what we do. For instance, extramarital affairs can threaten our partner's physical health and emotional dignity. When it's not a good idea to act out the fantasy, living it in our imagination can be just as illuminating and freeing as the act itself. If we suppress our desires, we starve the soul of expression; if we give them free rein, we risk overstepping the boundaries that keep us and others safe. We need not choose one or the other but can simply be conscious observers, acting only when it's clear we do so out of love. When we are honest about what ignites us, we can follow the soul's guidance into those places that await illumination, unlocking the very essence of who we are.

Let's take a closer look at what your sexual life might be showing you. If you let yourself be honest with the following exercise, you may discover something valuable about yourself.

What My Sexuality Says

1. I like sex because _____ .

2. What I don't like about it is _____

_____ .

3. In anticipation of having sex the feelings that arise are _____ .

4. My fantasies are _____ .

5. When I think of expressing them to my partner I feel _____.

6. I don't want to act them out because ____

_____.

7. If I looked deeply into my fantasies, they
would show me _____.

8. What is running through my mind during sex
is _____.

9. I really believe that sex is _____

_____.

10. If my partner knew _____,
she/he would _____.

Notice what comes up for you as you answer the questions. Can you see how sex can be such a useful gateway
to the innermost part of yourself?

If passion allows us to express ourselves in ways we
didn't know were possible or see ourselves from an altogether fresh perspective, when there is *not* sexual fire in
a relationship, it can feel empty in ways we can't ignore.
This too needs to be looked at and learned from. You
might ask what you are so attached to in your partner
that you are willing to sacrifice sexual connection for it.
Perhaps it's money or security. Or perhaps the fear of being alone in the world rules your decision to stay with
someone who doesn't appeal to you sexually. Or maybe
sex is scary because you don't feel comfortable with your

body. Whatever the case may be, if you are willing to be honest with yourself, you can see where you might be stuck or afraid and then move to open up. Again, arriving at an understanding and then accepting yourself are vital to spiritual growth. Rather than judge your decisions or thoughts about sex, you might instead see the places within you that need attention. Here are some questions to ask yourself if you don't feel sexual chemistry in your relationship.

A Question of Chemistry

1. Do I feel physical attraction for my partner? If not, how does it make me feel that the chemistry isn't there?
2. What initially drew me to my partner? What keeps me there?
3. Does my attachment (her money, his caretaking, my fear of being alone, our friendship, common goals, etc.) to my partner serve my spiritual growth?
4. What do I get out of the relationship?
5. What am I sacrificing?
6. Is it worth it?
7. For my part, do I remain in the relationship out of fear or is there genuine love? Which is the overriding force?

8. How do my partner and I serve each other in spiritual terms?

9. Can I come to terms with a partnership that has no chemistry? If so, how would I do that? If not, what do I foresee happening?

10. Am I willing to reprioritize in terms of what is important or am I satisfied with the way things are?

11. Am I on a soulful path?

12. Am I respecting my partner and honoring what we have?

13. What do I need to do or shift in order to become a more wholly integrated person?

There is no right way to answer; the questionnaire is designed only to make you *think*. It's amazing how sometimes we simply don't want to let our minds go to certain places for fear that we might shake up our world in ways we can't handle. But the only way to remain firmly on our spiritual path is to stay honest and be willing to adjust according to what we believe has integrity. Not everyone wants or needs sex; we are all motivated by different things at various times in our lives. But if we do want it and don't have it, we need to see what stands in the way and deal with it. Once again, sexuality is a doorway into the Self, but it is not the only one. Quiet walks and shared families and common goals create connections too. And when these are present and the magic of attraction cycles through our lives, we can be lifted and illuminated in ways we never thought possible.

I am not a sex therapist, but I can tell you that the better you know yourself, the more richly you will experience the sexual spectrum of love. How can you be fully alive if parts of you remain submerged and untouchable? To awaken passion in its most divine sense, we need to accept the many parts of our whole self. To know the ecstasy of the One, we must embrace and love all that is within us.

Staying Focused

Finding love is important, to be sure; but nurturing it so that it gets better is where soul work comes into play. Being in a relationship is a journey into consciousness; our weaknesses and strengths become clear as we travel. The partner we have chosen—or will choose—reflects our deeply held beliefs and desires. There are no mistakes, only revelations for the finding. When things are "good," the partnership is both an inspiration and a safe and supportive backdrop as we motor along in our lives. When things get "bad," it is most assuredly a catalyst to wake us up. Contrary to popular belief, the goal is not to be comfortable but to *stay conscious throughout whatever comes up* so that our spiritual growth remains our first priority. When we hold to our intention of experiencing soulful love, we can navigate the sometimes perilous storms thrown up by the ego.

Everything is always changing; we are subtly shifting and responding to life all the time. Children, jobs, and external events are constantly affecting the temperature of our partnership. Life is bound to throw us a few wrenches, and our relationships are bound to be challenging. Remember, if a relationship serves the higher good of everyone involved, it will thrive. If it doesn't, it will naturally lose steam and drop away. Whenever you feel unsure of your place in the partnership or wonder how to deal with something, consider turning to the following list I have put together to help keep moving in the right direction. The rules will assist you in nurturing the love you have—whether it is with someone you just met or an existing long-term relationship—and will help you smooth out the rough spots along the way.

Ten Rules to Live and Love By

1. See your partner through the lens of love rather than fear.

2. Be willing to forgive yourself and your partner, and to make amends when necessary.

3. Relax when times get tough; assume that "this too shall pass."

4. See in the dynamic of the relationship the reflection of what you need to learn.

5. When you don't know how to handle a problem, pray and meditate, surrendering the decisions to Spirit.

6. Honor your partner's path and allow them the
space to find their own way.

7. Keep up your personal growth work.

8. Follow the path of your own creativity.

9. Stay present.

10. Be grateful.

Let's go through each of these.

**Seeing your partner through the lens of love
rather than fear** automatically elevates the relationship to
a higher plane. When you can get quiet and note when you
are projecting fear, you can make the adjustment to see
through a different filter. So often we feel indignant or in-
censed, but upon closer inspection we will find that we are
really afraid. Once we assume our partner's core goodness
rather than focusing on their "guilt," they will be more free
to show us their best, which accelerates the process of shifting our perspective from one of blame and anxiety to one
of acceptance and peace. We can tap into the highest part
of ourselves by *acting as if* we are our most evolved self.

**Being willing to forgive yourself and your partner
and then making amends when necessary** is an ongo-

ing process of cleanup. We all make mistakes; it's human. But when we hold fast to a grudge, it eats away at our sense of peace and serenity. If you aren't willing to forgive, you might ask yourself what habit of ego you're attached to. Do you want to continue your life with unresolved issues hanging over you? When we take a stand and refuse to let go of something, we can always find evidence to justify it. Or we can try to make peace. Instead of blaming or making excuses, we can clean things up and move forward. This is not an excuse for staying in a dysfunctional situation, but an opportunity to see innocence. Once we do that, we gain—or give—freedom to move out of a "stuck" place.

The same attitude should be applied to our own shortcomings. We need to do the best we can, but when we fall short, instead of hating ourselves for it, we can ask for spiritual assistance to help us transform old patterns of behavior. Amends and forgiveness go hand in hand with spiritual evolution.

Relaxing when times get tough, assuming that "this too shall pass" allows you to roll with the punches. If you know things will inevitably arise to challenge you, you can be more detached when they do. Problems become worse when we dig in our heels and try to force a solution. By relaxing into whatever struggle arises, we remain flexible and open to inspiration and insight. Even if you have a hard time letting go, you can at least *observe* yourself taking things very seriously, which in itself helps to detach you from the experience of anxiety. Whatever is happening now won't be happening a year from now, so just keep breathing through the situation and see if you can take things a little less seriously.

Seeing in the dynamic of the relationship the reflection of what you need to learn helps bring you back to what is important. Sometimes we get lost in the chatter of day-to-day patterns and lose sight of the soul's mandate to bring us closer to realizing our Oneness. The best way to see where we need to work on things is to observe who we are and what we do within the context of a relationship. Any time you recognize your impulse to create distance rather than intimacy, you can make the adjustment and get back on track. This relationship, as with all relationships, is part of a curriculum to evolve into our highest potential. We come to know ourselves by how we interact with our partner, and by so doing, we come to know Spirit.

When you don't know how to handle a problem, praying and meditating aligns your limited energy with that which is all-powerful. Of course we don't have all the answers, but by consigning our limitations to our Higher Power, our burden is lifted. We need to be accountable for our words and actions and be willing to work through where we are stuck. We need to stay present and forgive. But beyond that, our creative power is fueled by Spirit. By praying, we ask for help and guidance;

by meditating, we clear our minds so that the answer will become apparent. By moving aside, we create an opening for God to work miracles in ways we could never imagine.

Honoring your partner's path and allowing them the space to find their own way sends a clear message of respect. People need to work things out in their own manner and in their own time. If you try to help where help is not requested, you are signaling your lack of belief in your partner. If you back off and assume someone is strong and intelligent, strength and intelligence are what they will likely find. Although we are all on this path of realization and expansion together, each of us is unique in our lessons to be learned; the way you do something might be totally different than how someone else needs to process a situation. Rest assured that Spirit is at work in all of our lives, and give yourself a rest from overseeing your partner's personal business.

Keeping up your personal growth work means you will keep your mind sharp and your awareness keen. Read, study, and attend lectures; don't rest on the laurels of what you think you already know. The moment we think we have it all figured out is the moment things will come crashing down around us. Arrogance leaves no room for intimacy or growth, and is certainly not part of a spiritual curriculum. When you immerse yourself in learning, you will always have new skills and interests to apply to a relationship, and thus the relationship will always feel fresh and relevant.

Following the path of your own creativity keeps you attuned to that which moves and inspires you. As you indulge your creative side, you become less dependent on your partner to feel whole. Creative energy is the force that breaks new ground. To sustain love, we need to continually fuel whatever inspires us on the deepest level. Also, creativity balances out the egoic and intellectual side of life; it teaches us to play and have fun. When we engage our passions, we radiate passionate energy and thus maintain the interest of our partner as well as having our own sense of fulfillment.

Staying present keeps us in the moment which is where life is. Life does not exist in future predictions or past grievances; all we have for sure is right here and right now. Every moment teaches us something, and if we are busily trying to change or control something, we miss the grace intended for us. By allowing the sacred mystery to unfold without trying to tamper with it, we can move through anything with much more ease and simplicity. As we cease resisting, any so-called negative situation or emotion will have the space to work out. And by the same token, when we are completely alert and aware in any given moment, we are open to the subtle miracles happening all around us. By staying present, we will see our partner for who they are; we will hear clearly their communication and respond to it astutely.

Being grateful for what you have zeros in on what is working, which in turn magnetizes more of the same. Where you put your focus is where you direct your creative intention; so if you want abundance, be grateful for your current wealth. If you want good health, be grateful for the vitality you have now. If you want a soulful relationship, be grateful for the soulful moments. Gratitude is like a seed you plant; it grows more as it is watered and nourished. Show your partner what you appreciate in them and let them know that they have a positive effect in your life. The acknowledgment of good will call forth more of the same.

As all of these principles become integrated into your romantic life, you will begin to notice an almost mystical and more soulful connection with your partner. The desire for something more or better will be superseded by the realization that what you have is already sublime in its own unique and purposeful way.

By now you can clearly see that love cannot be controlled or dictated; instead it is sourced by the authenticity we tap into as we build spiritual character. What we can access within ourselves, we can connect to in another. There is no perfect relationship to seek after, no way of making something fit into our fantasies; there is only a moment-by-moment identification with either the ego or grace. Thus, being in a relationship is a powerful practice as we move along our path to enlightenment. This is our doorway into Self-realization, an opportunity for salvation. We are here to transform, to take all that is fearful within us and replace it with love. When we feel deeply for someone, we are accomplishing our greatest work. When we honor that connection to another person, we are honoring Spirit.

chapter six

Handling Crises

Where one sees nothing but the One, hears nothing but the One, knows nothing but the One—there is the Infinite. Where one sees another, hears another, knows another—there is the finite. The Infinite is immortal, the finite is mortal.

It is written, He who has realized eternal Truth does not see death, nor illness, nor pain; he sees everything as the Self, and obtains all.

—CHANDOGYA UPANISHAD 7.23, 27

Inevitable in any relationship are the unforeseen events, challenges, or crises that will arise and need to be dealt with. Whether they take the form of infidelity, illness, or just spikes in the overwhelming pressures of daily life, we will be forced to face the unexpected. To put it unpoetically, *stuff happens*. And here too there is a gift, a lesson to be learned, even if not until you can look back on it. And although you can't control what happens to you, your response to it can have a big impact on how much suffering it brings.

People on a spiritual path have a tendency to believe that if they do everything right, bad things won't happen. And it's true that we co-create our world, so how we apply our free will *does* make an enormous difference. But there are also things that are beyond our control; some things may be destiny, some may be karma, and some are just plain impossible to understand while we are in the midst of them.

We can rail against events, crying that life is unfair, and we certainly have a right to those feelings. But after the initial reaction, we can take each moment as it comes and surrender to it, finding our way by listening to the sometimes gentle and sometimes powerful recognition of Spirit's voice within, guiding and prompting us to our highest potentiality. Mahatma Gandhi put it beautifully when he said, "The divine music is incessantly going on within ourselves, but the loud senses drown the delicate music, which is unlike and infinitely superior to anything we can perceive with our senses." A guiding wisdom lies within us, and we can tap into it if we turn away from the "loud senses" —even for just a moment—and go inside.

Below, I've addressed a few all-too-common crises. Some will look familiar, others not. In any event, remember this: no situation, as bad as it may seem at the time, is the end of the world. With God in our hearts, we can get through anything.

The Affair

Temptation. In almost every relationship, there will come a day when you question your commitment. You love your partner, but things may have gotten boring. Or predictable. Or tiring. Or maddening. And along comes someone who bowls you over with a magic you haven't felt in a long while, and suddenly life is rich and colorful again. What do you do? How do you handle an attraction that seems so overpowering? How can you not follow such a strong connection and see where it goes? When these questions arise in a relationship, they threaten the very foundation on which partnership is built: trust, integrity, and communication. And yet we have to respond, in some way, to the insistent tug on our hearts, and spirits, to try something new.

If you are tempted to have an affair, be aware that this too is an opportunity to expand your consciousness. Expanding your consciousness may be the last thing you're thinking of when lust is singing your name, but here, too, emerging consciousness is the bottom line. Remember, *chemistry is God's way of pulling you into a situation that will ultimately deliver you to some sort of awakening.*

Most everyone is presented with the temptation to stray at one time or another. It isn't wrong, and it doesn't make you a bad person to consider it. Monogamy is challenging, to say the least, because there are so many different aspects of ourselves that it's nearly impossible to be satisfied and fulfilled by one person over many years. But as you know by now, our partners are not in our lives only to satisfy and fulfill us; they serve a much higher calling. In addition to bringing us great joy, they are here to help advance us on the soul's journey to enlightenment.

As we navigate the various trials of a committed relationship, we are meant to be challenged and inspired to refine our higher instincts. How we behave with a partner helps us to see what we are made of and where our character could use some work. So a potential affair, even though it may seem threatening to our good spiritual image, also provides that perfect recipe for demanding our attention so that we can move more deeply into our inner work. Once again we are called upon to see if we can act in a compassionate and wise way, or if we are still attached to the more selfish ideals of ego. Intellectually, we may know what is right, but can we walk the walk? Nothing puts our feet to the fire more than wanting someone with all our heart and yet weighing the consequences in a soulful way.

Meeting someone you are very attracted to wakes up parts of yourself you may have forgotten existed. The feelings that were stirred in the beginning of your committed relationship might have been wonderful too, but if you haven't been very mindful of keeping things fresh, they probably mellowed out once you settled into your life and got caught up in the concerns of everyday living. Your world—both inner and outer—can suddenly be turned upside down and inside out by considering an affair. What an ideal looking-glass in which to take a closer look at who you are and what you are here to do! Sometimes things need to be shaken up so that all the pieces can come together in a new and more refined way.

Forbidden love—the desire to be with someone you are not "allowed" to be with—stirs that unfulfilled and empty part of yourself that you may have forgotten was even there. You may have a nice house, a fine marriage, and a good job, but when a new person brings about that exhilarating buzz, everything you have seems to pale in comparison with what you now so intensely desire. And that desire is precisely what you want to look at and focus on, because that longing is often a *spiritual hunger* at work. It is an inner awareness that things could be better, or at least different than they are right now.

Sometimes, craving change is healthy because it spurs us to action and makes us reach for something greater within ourselves and in our relationships. Leaning toward having an affair points up a serious inner turmoil that should not be ignored. Again, the soul is nudging us to wake up; it's time to break out of a holding pattern that we've outgrown and make a move. But what move? Before actually leaping into an affair, we would be wise to look squarely at the seed of our discontent. What are we missing? What are we trying to break away from? How can we address our needs and desires *while remaining* in the relationship? These are the questions we need to mull over and meditate on while our racing emotions fight the reins of restraint.

If we heed this wake-up call soulfully, we can use it to open our hearts and minds, which will often bring us back to nourish the relationship we're in. If we know things can be better, we should push for that. We can engage the strong emotions that arise from temptation and listen to what they are telling us. It is beholden on us to push through barriers that restrict love, and do so in accordance with the spiritual principles of kindness, compassion, and respect. In other words, you wouldn't go to your partner and say, "Hey, you don't turn me on anymore; what are we going to do about it?" You might instead approach the subject gently with, "I am feeling disconnected from you, and I am concerned that we won't be able to find our way back to each other if we let this go on much longer. I am even feeling tempted to find connection elsewhere. I am telling you this out of a genuine desire to make it work between us. Would you be open to working on this in a way we haven't yet tried?" This way, you are doing everything you can to try to head off the affair. You are trying to make things good at home before turning elsewhere.

At this point, let me assure you that simple self-restraint is only a stopgap measure. I could tell you to "just say no," but that would leave you with a truncated experience of love. If we want deep and meaningful relationships, we must know ourselves. I don't believe we can just turn away from an avenue of self-exploration—especially something as powerful as romantic chemistry—without really understanding what goes on beneath the surface. So let's continue.

As counterintuitive as it may sound, if you want to move out of the crisis you must *surrender* to it. By this I mean saying, "Okay, I see where we are. I am having these feelings. I am scared. I am at a crossroads. And I don't yet know what to do about it. I am willing to stay present with these feelings, and I am asking to be guided by Spirit to whatever course would be best for all involved." Remember, even as co-creators of our lives, sometimes we just have to let things unfold moment by moment. Which way to go will become apparent as we let ourselves experience the feelings that arise. We've seen that feelings, like anger, grow stronger if we try to resist them. So if we resist feeling attracted to someone, that attraction will surely grow, but when we let ourselves experience whatever feelings come up, they can move through us more readily, rather than become obsessive.

Once you've tuned in to the inner workings of your heart and mind, consider the reality of following through on your desire to go outside the relationship. Think it through. Imagine it. How would it feel? Consider all the consequences. Be realistic.

Wanting someone to satisfy your longings and make you feel alive is the ego's response to a spiritual call. It may do the trick for a little while, as you plug into something that seems "bigger than both of you." But in all likelihood, the new love will end up being a let down. All too often I see friends and clients follow their impulses into a wild, tempestuous affair with claims of "this is really *it*." They have incredible sex, become fit and trim almost overnight, and swoon at each other's every gesture. But after some time passes, the newness wears off, issues arise, and the magic starts to evaporate in the presence of everyday life. They begin to miss the stability and comfort of their committed partner. Or guilt and confusion drive them to exhaustion and self-loathing. Although considering an affair is exciting and intriguing, the reality of it doesn't fill that deep yearning, at least not for long. And that's when things get messy.

What's missing for each of us can't be found in a person (as much as we project our dreams on them); it is instead a *connectedness with Spirit* that we look for in the new liaison. We hunger to feel that sense of excitement, of unlimited possibility, that so intoxicated us when we first met our current partner. But the truth is, as time passes, it becomes evident that the new lover is only human, has their own garden-variety shortcomings, and probably cannot take us where we want to go any better than our current (or now former) partner. For a short while we can take a wild and intriguing ride and feel profoundly connected; but unless we are acting in fundamentally new ways—seeing perfection instead of fault, forgiving, and acting lovingly—we will come around to the same old state of mind. And look to the next affair for salvation.

People will forever disappoint us when we look only to them to provide us with a sense of well-being. And the soul, in its infinite wisdom, will always disabuse us of the notion that true happiness can be ours if we can only find the just-right person. The "perfect" person is never perfect. Perfection lies in the perception, and that comes from us. The responsibility of experiencing happiness rests with us and our ability to perceive Spirit in everyone, especially the one with whom we are significantly involved.

If we don't have an authentic sense of spiritual connection in our lives, we will always come up feeling empty and dissatisfied—first with our committed partner, and then with a new partner. If we long for something deep and sacred but chase after the transient intrigue of an affair, we will have missed the mark. Feeling "plugged in" as a result of a new experience can only be temporary; but by its failure to please in a sustaining way it will actually point us to the real source.

The longing we experience—and often mistake as a

need to be with a new person—is our human need to bond, to join together, to *relate*. Even though it may look and feel like good old-fashioned body heat, at a deeper level we are essentially being drawn to dissolve the sense of separation between ourselves and God by experiencing *connection*. The body is articulating our inherent spiritual aspirations. Its impulse is undeniably real and cannot be ignored, but if we go about acting on it thoughtlessly— indulging in the appeal of something new without considering our current situation fully—we can cause a lot of unnecessary pain. I'm not saying don't act; I am saying think deeply about your motivation and how your actions would affect everyone involved. Think of what you are trying to accomplish in your life and in your relationships, and then consider the most effective way of going about it. When you slow down enough to think clearly, chances are you will reconsider jumping ship.

Our soul nudges us to experience our depth of being and that can take some time; but the ego seeks instant gratification. We long to make a connection, but as the song says, we're "looking for love in all the wrong places." Yes, we can find a spiritual connection with someone new, but unless we are consistently moving to support our spiritual nature, we will get disappointed time and again. Eventually we will realize that our true nature requires of us that we love with all our heart that one to whom we have committed—that we give them all we have until it becomes apparent there is nothing more that serves our higher growth. Then, and only then, is it time to move on and entertain something new.

What you can do instead of having an affair is to *feel* the longing and know that it is a call for Spirit to move through and with you. Then consent to being completely present, open, and aware; offer yourself and the outcome up to the guidance of Spirit and let things unfold accordingly.

Ask yourself what the most spiritual response to the situation in question would be. I can't tell you what the answer will look like. You may be inspired to be more forthcoming in your marriage (or current partnership), to express yourself more openly. You may realize you haven't given your partner a chance to see the real you, nor have you invited them to show you their inner life. Or you may realize you would no longer be acting with integrity by staying in a relationship that has long since reached its limit. Only you can see what is called for at this time. Let your longing pull you to the wisdom that is waiting to be tapped. Rather than act impulsively or condemn yourself for "impure" thoughts, listen to the still-small voice that has been aroused in you. Let it guide you into your Self and then the decisions will become clear.

Even though it is hard to face, sometimes a relationship will come to its natural end. You might have learned from and grown with your partner as much as was possible. Perhaps the potential affair serves as the necessary impetus to finally see the wisdom in moving on. Pain is a warrior of Spirit; it comes crashing through the walls of ego so that we wake up. And by *feeling* so intensely, we open our hearts to Spirit, if from nothing else than utter desperation.

But what if you are the one from whom your partner has strayed? How do you know if you should leave or try and rebuild?

Meet Patty, a client who came to me after she found out her husband had been having an affair. Patty and Greg lived in a lovely suburban enclave where their kids were free to run around to their friends' houses. It was the kind of place where the neighbors were friendly and regularly got together for barbeques and softball games. Patty's next-door neighbor, in particular, was very close to them. If Patty and Greg went out of town, Scarlett would pick up their mail and feed the cats for them. Because she didn't have kids of her own and her husband was on the road most of the time, Scarlett had plenty of time to babysit the twins when Patty had to run errands, and every Friday night Scarlett would bring over a pot of her famous three-bean chili to share in front of the TV.

Patty was very pleased that she had someone she could hang out with, and was happy that Greg had someone to go running with in the evenings when he got home from work. She knew he enjoyed jogging with another person to break the monotony of his long runs. Even though she had never lost the weight she gained from carrying her daughters, Patty just couldn't force herself to keep up with Greg's fitness program. He was a gym teacher, and sometimes she felt he regarded her as the assistant coach who never quite ran a tight enough ship.

One Saturday afternoon, Patty was opening up the mail while Greg was watching a football game. Her jaw dropped as she read through a letter that had been addressed to her and signed anonymously. Apparently, one of the neighbors who really liked Patty wanted her to know what was going on behind her back. This neighbor had glimpsed Greg and Scarlett one time too many ducking into a house down the street that was under construction. Curious, and more than a little nosy, the neighbor walked over and snuck inside to see Greg and Scarlett in a naked embrace. This neighbor didn't say anything at first, but came to the conclusion that Patty should know so she could protect herself against this woman who had become so much a part of her household.

Hysteria rising up in her chest, Patty flung the letter into Greg's lap and demanded to know what the hell was going on. After hours of both partners screaming and crying, Greg finally admitted to the affair. He said he was wrong and that he was sorry, but then swiftly moved into his defense. "How can you expect me to not have sex for weeks at a time? I got sick and tired of trying to get my own wife into bed. Every time I tried to touch you, you turned away, or acted like you were doing me a big favor, so I stopped trying. I don't need to feel this unappreciated in my own home. It was wrong, what I did, and I hope you can forgive me. But I didn't sign up for a sexless marriage."

Patty was stunned. She had thought maybe Greg wouldn't notice that she wasn't that into sex. She figured that once she lost some weight and the twins got a little older, she would get back into feeling more connected to her husband. She had been afraid to admit to him that she was feeling insecure and overwhelmed; instead she hoped that one day things would just work themselves out. In any case, this was not an acceptable excuse for what had happened.

At this point in the retelling of her story, I asked Patty what was coming up for her, what emotions lay beneath her description of events. The first word that came to her was rage. She was furious at Greg, and out of her mind with rage at Scarlett, whom she had regarded as her friend. After she did a good bit of venting, I asked her what else, if anything, she was angry about. Out poured everything she had been carrying around without even knowing it. She was angry that she didn't have any time to herself, angry that her body wasn't trim anymore. She was angry that Greg acted just like another child who needed to be fed and supported and stroked and cleaned up after. She was angry that her life had started to look a whole lot like that of her parents: her mother ran around and took care of everything to the point of exhaustion, while her father did whatever he pleased. And even though Patty had always encouraged her mom to take better care of herself and have some fun with friends, she never could seem to step away from the demands of five children and an overbearing husband.

Then the tears came. Patty said it was strange, but she had known something terrible would happen. She felt like she was at her limit, and something would have to give. She had been living in fear that she was not "enough" to handle her life and she was buckling under the weight of her responsibilities. Her mother had died of breast cancer five years ago and Patty secretly suspected that the stress her mother was constantly under had caused the disease and she feared that would also be her fate.

At this point, I told Patty that as terrible as it all seemed, there was a reason for what transpired. I assured her that she would get through the crisis, but that what was essential was that she start listening to those parts of herself she had been trying to keep controlled and silenced. Patty needed to process some anxieties that dated back to her childhood. She needed to allow herself to feel the fear and rage so that those emotions could get unstuck and no longer attract events that demanded Patty's attention. I explained to her that her soul was trying to break her out of some historic family assumptions (that the woman in the family had to sacrifice for the man; that life was difficult and unrewarding; that sex was something you did just to keep your man quiet; that it was good to have a "nice" life and not rock the boat). I encouraged Patty to take this time to get to know what was going on inside her and assured her that as she did this, eventually the answers about what to do would become clear.

Patty decided to stay in her home but asked Greg to take an apartment for a month or two while she figured out what she wanted to do. Because he was intent on keeping his family together, Greg made a vow never to see Scarlett again. And because gossip has a way of getting around, Scarlett's husband also found out about the affair. Within days, the two of them packed up and left the neighborhood, thankfully relieving Patty of running into her former friend.

Patty undertook a program aimed at really coming to know herself. She listened to her Dark Voice and allowed all sorts of emotions and thoughts to surface. She took long walks and talked to God, sometimes raging and sometimes sobbing, until things began to shift in her. She noticed that her journal entries were becoming more about her own inner life than about Greg and what he did. She started feeling compassion for herself rather than just frustration. She saw where her marriage had become less about love and more about appearances. And she began to feel some hope.

To make a long story short, Patty and Greg decided to stay together. They embarked on couple's therapy and even went away for a weeklong seminar on building a more intimate relationship. Things were not easy for the first year, but slowly they came to see each other in new ways. They committed to continue working individually on their issues, and after a while, they became closer than ever. Patty's willingness to give her marriage another try came from realizing that what happened actually "cracked her open" and was, in some way, a blessing. She no longer felt the burden of her mother's way of doing things and concluded that she could break free from her family legacy.

The key to dealing with any crisis is to listen to your intuition and heed its wisdom. As you come to know yourself and your inner workings, grace will reveal itself and light the way. And as we change, the world around us can't help but change as well.

Should you be faced with a situation like Patty's or Greg's, here are some questions to help focus your mind.

Questions to Ask When Facing Infidelity

1. What am I learning by going through this?
2. In what ways does the affair (or potential to have an affair) bring me closer to the truth I was not willing to see?

3. Where am I not being loving (to myself and my partner), and how can I change that?

4. What beliefs are being challenged?

5. Where do I need to let go?

6. Where do I need to practice discipline?

7. What qualities are trying to emerge in me? What is my soul guiding me to learn?

8. Do I believe in my heart that I deserve happiness? If so, what shall I do?

9. Am I treating my partner with respect and honor?

10. Am I fully present to all of my feelings?

These are important considerations. Again, there is no one-size-fits-all answer. For some, the best thing might be to leave and move on. For others, the partnership can emerge stronger than ever by staying and working things through. Even though an affair is painful, it provides a huge opportunity for insight and healing if we hold to growth as our prime intention. Sometimes what we think is killing us is actually illuminating aspects of ourselves we never knew existed.

I am often asked if I think people can change. Can a cheater stop cheating? Can a liar stop lying? Yes, of course they can; but it will be an enormous undertaking and it takes immense spiritual dedication to evolve beyond well-established patterns. All too often, people stick to their way of relating until they are forced by crisis to snap out of it. It takes a fierce honesty and willingness to delve into the inner workings of the psyche to begin to transform. Not everyone is up for the challenge, but spiritual evolution is the very reason we are here. I certainly encourage the effort.

So how do we know if it's time to leave? There is hardly anything more difficult or heart-wrenching than the decision to end a relationship, so that decision should be made with as much love and detachment as possible. When there is still a heavy charge—fury or indignation—in the relationship, you might do well to consider the possibility that it is not yet finished; there still might be emotional issues to contend with in the context of the relationship. Here are a few ways you can tell you are not ready to end things.

It's Not Yet Finished If . . .

1. You are still outraged at your partner and are unwilling to do some work with your feelings.
2. You insist that your partner take full responsibility for what happened.
3. If you have children, you can see how they are being negatively affected, yet you can't stop fighting.
4. Instead of focusing on your own healing, you tell anyone who will listen how you were wronged.

5. You haven't changed or grown from the situation.

If any of these statements seems to resonate, you are not ready to move on (assuming you have a choice); you are still attached to the dynamic of your relationship. What we are attached to—even if it is a negative attachment—is what we pull into our lives and keep re-creating. It becomes our calling card, our identity. As unnerving as it is to be faced with the crisis of loyalty, it is bringing up something you should carefully explore. Perhaps you need to come to terms with old anger, or perhaps deceit brings up issues of low self-esteem. But whatever the affair brings up for you, listen. If you don't take responsibility in some way, you will remain powerless to change anything. Pay attention. And then move to heal the wound.

Until you can eventually see the situation calmly and claim your learned lessons, it would be wise to reinvigorate your commitment to work on yourself. If you don't take the opportunity now to emotionally connect to your inner life, you will likely create a similar event in the future that will be even more trying. If it works for you, think of the situation as an experiment. Use the pain or frustration as a signal to go deeper; don't walk away without learning what your soul is trying to teach you.

Remember, the people who come into our lives (no

matter what form they take) are healers; they are showing us where we could use some spiritual scrutiny. If you
allow the present situation to enrich you, it will turn out
to have been a perfect relationship after all.

Here are a few ways you can tell if you are free to
move on.

You Are Free to Move on If . . .

1. You wish your partner well, genuinely hoping
   they are happy and that their life is fruitful.
2. You see that both of you want different things
   out of life, and accept that.
3. You want to take from your combined assets
   only what you feel, unemotionally, has been
   earned by you.
4. If you have children, they notice peace between Mom and Dad and feel, for the most
   part, secure.
5. Your creativity is sparked more by leaving
   than staying.
6. You feel sad and grieve the loss of the relationship, but the pain is assuaged by a deep sense
   that this is the right thing to do.

If the above statements resonate for you, kudos to you.
You have taken a difficult situation and let it shape you

into someone who is wise, seasoned, and ready to move forward. You have worked through enormous emotional turmoil and you have stayed the course, looking within and doing the work of the spiritual warrior.

If you are somewhere between not yet finished and moving on, hang in there. Keep your heart open and the energy moving. Things take time to become clear, but they will if we want them to. The decision to stay in or leave a relationship is immensely important in the spiritual journey. Think carefully about your motivations, and after taking an emotional inventory of what is yours to own, let your decision come in its own time. If you can, talk with a counselor or trusted friend with whom you can explore your thoughts and sound out where your heart is. Sometimes simply hearing yourself speak helps to sort things out.

Whatever you decide to do, treat your partner with respect (even if it is not reciprocal) and share your business only with those who have some direct reason for being involved. And throughout it all, engage regularly in quiet meditation, allowing yourself to be led by Spirit. You will be inspired as to which way to go and how to go about it.

Chronic Stress

We usually think of a crisis as a sudden, shocking event that stops us in our tracks. But there is also another

kind of crisis, which sneaks up slowly and unnoticed until things get so strained we realize we're on the brink of
losing our minds—and maybe our relationship as well.
The pressure to keep pace with an ever more demanding
world is overwhelming, not to mention that it leaves us
with little or no attention left over to give to the sacred.
Frenzy pushes us to neglect the big picture, and when we
do, the relationship will almost certainly run into trouble.
It may be mounting credit card debt or impossible work
demands. It could be little things that add up or some
huge catastrophe that pushes us over the edge. Whatever
it is though, if it is not dealt with appropriately, the re-
sulting stress will become chronic.

Stress is contagious; everyone around the revved-up,
strung-out person feels the pressure. Stress is addictive too.
We can get hooked on the adrenaline and it's almost as if we
don't feel fully alive unless we're in a constant stream of
new dramas. Some of us unconsciously gravitate toward
chaos, or create it, so we can keep ourselves in a heightened
state. We are in fight mode, which is certainly far from love
or receptivity. Or we are in flight mode, shut down to each
other while we attend to whatever demands our attention.
We start feeding off of fear and anxiety rather than nurturing ourselves with periods of quiet serenity. If we aren't
careful, stress becomes the way of our life.

When we are frenzied, our kids pick up on our energy
and they add to it with their own brand of craziness;

even animals have a way of absorbing the neurotic energy of their caretakers and then act in kind. At work there is an unspoken agreement that certain individuals (the so-called tireless ones) will pick up the slack; people can always, almost psychically, sense who among us is the willing scapegoat or the non-stop workhorse. At home we cease talking like lovers and instead treat each other as means to an end. And then one day we wake up to realize that our lives have careened out of control and that stress has delivered us into a full-on crisis.

How do we get back on track?

By slowing down and taking a deep breath, we can center our minds. We can decide to stop worrying, whether or not everything is getting done. And we can remind ourselves that although we are very powerful, we are not *all*-powerful. Stepping aside and inviting the grace of Spirit to enter into any situation makes room for all sorts of improvements to unfold in unexpected ways. And then one of two things will happen: either the things we stressed about will resolve without much effort, or we will finally be relaxed enough to hear solutions when they gently introduce themselves into our thinking.

But if we don't slow down and invite the grace of spiritual assistance into our hectic lives, things will only escalate. And one day that wake-up call will come in the form of illness, a mental breakdown, or our partner informing us they have had enough.

The effects of chronic stress on a relationship are well illustrated by the story of Dede and Rob. Dede was a highly successful businesswoman and the breadwinner of the family. Rob was in the early stages of his new business and was swamped on a daily basis. They also had quite a busy household with two teenagers at home. Dede was already under incredible pressure keeping up the pace at work, not to mention the added responsibilities of funding Rob's venture and paying the mortgage, private school tuition, and all the expenses a busy family incurs. She found herself taking on difficult clients that she normally wouldn't have just because of financial worries. But the straw that nearly broke the back of their marriage was the discovery that their young teenage daughter was using drugs and experimenting with sex.

"For the better part of two years, everything was about our daughter, Ella. We got her into a drug program and we all went into family therapy. The financial strain of that—about four thousand dollars a month—was another burden on me. Rob was emotionally handling things in his own way, but we didn't agree on a lot of issues and I began to shut him out. He was at the absolute bottom of my list; I was numbed to our relationship and I was sick of everything and everyone.

"I had gotten increasingly busy at work, and I will admit that my office was the only place I could forget about it all. And of course, I felt acutely responsible for Ella's drug problem. I hadn't been around enough to notice the changes in her, and I was angry at Rob for not getting his end together successfully enough so that I could have some time and space to devote to other things besides work. But after months and months of continuous dramas—Ella sneaking out and the cops delivering her to our doorstep stoned, for one—when Rob announced he was moving out, I just hit bottom. It felt like a giant tidal wave of pain and failure, and I thought I was going to die."

"I've never loved anyone more than Dede, but we had been living in an emotional wasteland. She never touched me and never turned to me for comfort. I felt as if I repulsed her. I was doing the best I could, but I wasn't generating the kind of money we needed, nor did I have the ability to help her out much. I missed her love and respect. And it wasn't Ella's fault. We were headed in this direction before she got in trouble. But once Ella's situation hit the fan, our marriage became an arctic zone. In times of trouble, you either turn to each other, or you turn away. Dede turned away, so I felt I had no other choice but to turn away too."

"When Rob announced he was moving out, I felt something spring to attention inside me, like I had been swimming around in turbulent waters but finally caught a glimpse of the shoreline. I did not want my marriage to end. I loved Rob, but I hadn't considered him a priority in a long time. I asked him to please stay, and I told him I wanted to work together to recapture what we once had, and maybe even make things better than ever. Thankfully, he agreed. We decided to recommit to our marriage. We gave ourselves some financial breathing room by moving out of the city and putting the kids into a lovely neighborhood school that had smaller classes and less exposure to big-city ways. I've learned to be less of a control freak at work, and I have eased up on the pressure on myself considerably; I delegate a whole lot more than I did before. I spend more time at home with my family, and I definitely take time to appreciate what I've got."

"Dede and I created this sort of ritual every morning before we hit the outside world; we hold hands for a minute and look into each other's eyes, saying, 'Whatever this day brings, we are in it together.'"

"It's a great way to start the day. And even though the pressures at work are still there, and Ella's sobriety is always tenuous, I am reminded every day by this little ritual I have with Rob that I am not in this life alone, and that the most important thing of all is the love we share. It may look like we have less from the outside—no more fancy house or car—but I think we both found so much serenity in realizing we don't need them like we thought we did. We all started doing twelve-step work—Ella went to Alateen so that she could deal with her addiction, and Rob and I went to Alanon so that we could find fellowship with other people dealing with similar issues. The great thing is that those programs are free, so it relieved the financial squeeze a bit; their main thrust is to remind us to 'Let go and let God,' which is what we continue to do to this day."

Dede and Rob's shift did not happen overnight, but they rose up and dealt with their challenges with love. They survived their slow-building crisis and ended up far better off for it.

Although it may sound antithetical to modern-day messages of empowerment, we are not meant to do it all; power and wealth are not necessarily signs of success. Life is not about climbing the job hierarchy or driving the flashiest car on your block. It's okay to work toward these things and appreciate them as they manifest, but they are just *backdrops* for the real purpose of our lives, which is to expand in our ability to love. We miss the point entirely if we get caught up in just trying to get things accomplished.

All the challenges we face are necessary so we can learn humility, be inspired to re-align our energy with Spirit, and surrender our ego's desires. So in times of stress and breakdown, slow down and tap into the inner stillness. Listen. We need to allow Spirit to flow through and transform us and the situations at hand. We need to remember to make love—and the soul mate relationship—a priority.

When you begin to slow down to get your bearings, you will probably find that you lost perspective. You might have expected things in your life to look a certain way and believed it was up to you to make that happen. But when you put too much stock in external aspects of life, you put your faith and energy into something fleeting and ultimately unfulfilling. I'm not saying don't take things seriously; jobs and kids and health are serious business, but the trick is to try to *find peace with the process of life* rather than with specific results. Listen to your intuition and relax a little more. Practice *allowing*.

Do what you can with the cards you are dealt, stay in touch with your feelings, and keep breathing through it all. Then move forward with awareness, authenticity, and integrity. And surrender. In other words, roll with it. Things may not always be to your liking, but try to assume there is a divine design at work.

The nature of life is that things are always changing. Nothing stays the same for long. After you get what you wanted you will realize it wasn't the needed salve after all. The children you longed for grow up and leave the nest; the job you thought had so much status isn't as prestigious as that next position on the organizational chart, and the house you counted on to make you happy never looks quite as perfect as the one in the magazine. Things are transient. People die. The price of getting by gets higher. Beauty fades, and life is always on the move. What makes you happy one day doesn't work so well the next, because *it's not supposed to*. As soon as we start to believe that an external factor is what life is all about, our Higher Power will bust us so that we'll know better.

We are meant to embrace our spiritual nature; it is the only way to sustain joy and a sense of meaning. If you are suffering from chronic stress, this is a lesson you have not yet learned.

Chronic stress can also be used to avoid the pain of depression. Depression, I believe, is often a spiritual crisis. Yes, some people have chemical imbalances that require medication, but to a large extent, we are a nation of people who have fallen out of touch with God. Some of us use food as a substitute, others use alcohol or drugs. And others yet use chaos and stress as an excuse to stave off dealing with the deep, inner issues that need attention. Here is a prayer I often use when I find myself getting frenzied or out of sorts.

Prayer for Stressful Times

God, please help me to be still so that I can feel your presence. Breathe your serenity into my being, remind me that I am in your care. Assist me in letting go of my need for control. Allow me to feel your peace. Move through me in ways that realign my will with yours. And deliver me to my highest potential in this and all of my affairs. Amen.

Chronic stress is a choice; we can make things easier if we want to. Simplicity is the lens through which Spirit sees everything: there is only love and everything else is an illusion. If we want to regain equilibrium, we need only shift our attention to this very moment and accept it. We can choose to love rather than rail against life. We can take things as they come and remember to keep surrendering.

There are times when you will feel pushed to accomplish more than you think you are capable of; this temporary stress can be useful. But at the end of the day be sure to put down your worldly concerns and refocus your mind on love. Nothing is so important that it should keep us from our journey to wholeness.

Illness or Injury

In a world racing at breakneck speed, illness or injury brings everything to a screeching halt. You may have thought you had concerns before, but when a medical crisis hits, everything else falls away. It's as if you were punched in the stomach. Stunned, you grapple with disbelief. "How can this happen?" "Why us?" "Why me?" But it *has* happened, and suddenly your life is altered in ways you could have never foreseen.

My father recently passed away at age sixty three, after

struggling with melanoma for five months. He had been having terrible headaches for a few weeks and could barely get out of bed. When my mother tried to help him to the bathroom, he fell down and passed out from the pain. At the emergency room they scanned his whole body and found a hemorrhaging mass in his brain the size of a tennis ball. Our family was frozen with fear and dread. The surgeon removed the tumor, and we were momentarily relieved that my father had made it through until we started researching brain metastasis from melanoma and realized how dire his situation was.

We kicked into high gear, my mother, two brothers and I, and set about doing everything in our power to save my father's life. I took control of his diet and stocked the house with organic fruits and vegetables, vitamins, and herbal supplements. One of my brothers found all sorts of alternative treatments on the Internet, while the other worked at getting all Dad's medical papers and documents in order. For the first few days my mother walked around like she had been hit by a Mack truck; she was unable to take in what was going on and, in between panic attacks, had gone numb with fear. I couldn't imagine how she must have been feeling watching the love of her life go through this. But neither could I imagine what my father must be feeling as his family circled around him, taking over all the various tasks he had so proudly performed all his life. Even as our roles came sharply into focus, the whole of our reality changed in an instant.

We made the rounds of oncologists, never quite getting a clear or hopeful path from any of them. Chemotherapy had shown promise, but it didn't increase his chances of survival. A vaccine had been approved, but it showed minimal success with brain tumors. Radiation might alleviate symptoms, but it would also affect motor skills and cognitive function. One day we had hope, and the next day it was dashed. As much as I wanted to believe that a miracle would save my father, there were no miracles in sight. Apparently, what Dad had was pretty deadly and there was not much time to change its course. He didn't know all this, but we did. He didn't ask what his chances were, nor did he read the research we'd collected, so we honored what seemed to be his decision not to hear bad news. He was also fairly opposed and overwhelmed by alternative therapies, and so we respectfully stopped pushing him to try new things.

I kept reminding myself that there was grace and wisdom to be found in everything, but I just couldn't see them in the emergency hospital visits and long sleepless nights talking Dad through the terrifying visions he was battling. Where was the grace in my father's suffering and pain, I wanted to know. What wisdom could justify his torment? I didn't have the answers but I was willing to surrender myself to a process that clearly was out of my control in hopes that things would unfold as they were supposed to.

I decided that all I could do, aside from staying on top of the doctors and nurses and running the necessary errands, was to be fiercely present to everything that arose, no matter how painful, and to respond with as much love and faith as I could muster. Even though I wanted to resist with all my heart the notion that my father could die, I allowed myself to feel the full brunt of fear and anguish so that I could empathize with him. I held my mother's hand as the realization that she was losing her lifelong partner sank in, and I forced myself to keep breathing. She couldn't do enough for him, and watching her run around taking care of Dad's every need broke my heart. I knew she felt responsible for making him feel better, and I knew it was beyond her ability to do so. But how do you tell someone whose whole life was wrapped up in her husband to let go? For her, that was an impossibility. And yet it was something she would have to come to do.

My dad was always the one in charge, always the go-to guy for questions of what to do and how to do it. Now suddenly my mom had to figure things out for herself; she was forced to start thinking in ways that were foreign to her, ways that she was not comfortable with. She had to be decisive and self-reliant, and more than anything, she had to start acknowledging some pretty painful feelings. And my father, too, began to surrender in ways he had never felt comfortable doing. He had no choice any-more; he had to. He could no longer power his way through a difficult situation, which he had always done before; he had to trust people to take care of him.

I think the most stunning realization for my father during this crisis was that he was deeply loved by so many people. He was a tough guy, fun loving, and always the life of the party, but I think he honestly didn't know that he was *loveable* before he got cancer. It rendered him speechless when the flowers and letters poured in. When friends took so much time out of their day to be with him in the hospital, he wondered if there wasn't something he had missed about himself, some good thing that he had not known of but was now being affirmed. This illness, this horrible curse that had befallen my family and Dad, oddly began to heal us all.

The story of my father's illness is a profound one (as is every story of loss), and one day I will write about it fully. But for the purposes of this book, I think it is sufficient to say that there is no way of knowing how grace will reveal itself; it does so in its own time. The miracles of healing aren't necessarily obvious when they occur; sometimes you just wake up one day to realize that you are a different person. Surely we would never choose this sort of pain, but once the pain presents itself, we have to walk hand in hand, as part-ners, friends, or family members into the fire of transfor-mation, allowing the Alchemist to shape us at His will.

During the ordeal with my father, I found that if I was not disciplined in my spiritual practice of staying present and loving, I could very easily be overwhelmed by fear, and so I've put together some questions to help focus your mind should you have to deal with illness or injury. By answering them, you will find yourself tuning into your spiritual stance. You will be better able to get through this trial and be of service to your partner if you are alert, aware, and in command of your intentions. Whether you are the patient or the caregiver, it is not about finding the *right* way of doing something to achieve a certain result, but rather how you might come into yourself—and assist your partner in doing the same—by walking through the fire and into the most intense intimacy you have ever known.

From the Fire, Gold

1. What do I feel right now? Can I allow for all of these feelings and go straight into the center of them?

2. What is this experience bringing up for me?

3. What are all the emotions my partner must be feeling? Am I being compassionate?

4. How can I be of service physically, emotionally, and spiritually?

5. What do I need to process separately from my partner? With whom and how can I do that so that it causes no additional pain or burden?

6. What am I seeing now that I would not have seen were it not for this crisis?

7. Who am I becoming, and what parts of me can I leave behind?

8. How can I express love in ways I could not before?

9. Can I let go of my attachment to what I want to have happen?

10. Am I completely present?

11. Am I willing to surrender all of this to God?

The answers won't come immediately, but these questions are designed to put your mind—and heart—in the right place. All we ever have is this very moment, so the only thing we can do for sure is *be present*. The more present you are, the richer your experience will be. Trauma may bring us to our knees, but our willingness to keep our hearts open will be the force that lifts us up.

Our agreement, as partners, is to be on this path together, to accompany each other through our ordeals. Knowing you aren't alone is a tremendous comfort. As we share an experience, we can give each other blessings to live—and even die—by. Even as we let go, we can embrace our interconnectedness with each other. The compassion that arises when we truly love one another is one of the greatest miracles a person can experience.

When my father passed, he was surrounded by his family as he left this earth, knowing he was deeply loved and appreciated. Through her grief my mother came to know her husband in ways she could not have imagined. Their bond was such that in the end their souls may have consented to a temporary parting, but I imagine they are still very much a part of each other. None of us will ever be the same after saying "good-bye" to this man who was so central to our lives, but I feel we were all touched in indescribably intimate ways for having gone through it together. My family, even in our anguish, experienced miracles we are still digesting. There was indeed wisdom and certainly grace, too.

Here is a visualization that can help to inject healing energy into a crisis caused by illness or injury. You may want to ask a friend to read it out loud to you if you are too out of sorts to take yourself through it. Remember to keep breathing, and remember to keep turning things over to God.

Meditation for Crises

Close your eyes and find your breath. Deepen your inhale as you imagine a beautiful soft light being drawn into your body. As you exhale, let go of your anxiety, your anguish. Take ten breaths this way, dropping down farther into the center of your being with each one.

Feel your whole body being soothed by this healing light.

Now call to your mind's eye an image of your life at this critical moment in time. Observe the panic. Notice the pain on the faces of your loved ones; feel the anguish in your own heart.

And then surrender all of it to Spirit, asking that everyone affected be lifted up and transformed by the love that shows itself as pure light.

Feel a sense of calm, knowing that everything will be OK.

Visualize each person feeling serene, even joyful. Feel as if the very best possibility is being manifested right now and that all is well.

And so it is.

When you feel a sense of completion, gently bring your breathing back to normal and open your eyes.

Success

If you are wondering how success could possibly be viewed as a crisis, just look at how frequently Hollywood stars break up, or the likelihood of a high-powered

CEO's being on their second or third spouse, or the disintegration of the personal lives of some Lotto winners. In twelve-step groups it is widely recognized that recovering addicts are just as likely to relapse from the onset of success as they are from losing a job or a loved one. This is because we take material success much too seriously in our society, ignoring that it tends to feed the ego self rather than the spiritual Self.

The more we buy into the ego's game of rating ourselves according to outward success, the more shallow and disengaged from our truth we become. There is nothing wrong with ambition as long as it is balanced with a solid, down-to-earth awareness that we are all equal in the eyes of God. Unfortunately, it's all too easy to get caught up in the pursuit of achievement and all the goodies that go along with worldly triumph. It is certainly challenging not to get addicted to ego gratification, but when you start believing in your own press, as they say, you are in trouble.

To achieve success, a lot of time and energy is required, which may tempt you to put the soul mate relationship and all its spiritual needs on the back burner. You can get so busy that you no longer honor the simple pleasures of partnership. You might forget to serve (and we *are* meant to serve) your partner because you are so busy serving a ballooning ego. When you get used to people deferring to you, it's easy to transfer the expectation of subservience to your partner. And the more successful you are, the less likely people will be to disagree with you. You risk losing touch with reality altogether.

As we climb the ladder of achievement, we need to remind ourselves of the reason we are alive. We are here to evolve, to love, and to support each other. Life is not about seeing how much money we can make or how many possessions we can acquire. It's not even about how many years we can stay married. As a matter of fact, those aspirations can really get in the way of *true* success, which can only be gauged by how diligently we have cleared the way for Spirit to move through us. By contrast, worldly success requires enormous dedication to the ego. Ego would have us believe that, to be successful, we have to choose materialism over compassion or kindness, which is never the case.

I find a tragic and heart-wrenching example of this in the way animals are used in commerce. In the name of increasing profits, animals are raised and slaughtered in ways that are brutal and inhumane. The ego says, "Never mind what the animals feel; let's just get on with this more efficiently so we can hit our numbers." But the soul whispers, "Wake up! Look at what you are doing and change your ways. Be kind." We are faced all the time with choices that will reflect who we are and how we are doing on a soulful level. Do we choose the job at the expense of a private life? Do we care more about profit than progress on

the spiritual path? The pressures of keeping up and winning can take every ounce of our focus if we let them. But
we cannot bargain with the force of evolution; if we aren't
going the way of our heart, things will begin to fall apart.
Not as punishment or retribution, but the crisis we will
find ourselves in will come about to shake us up, to edu-
cate us. It may be an emotional breakdown or it may be
physical illness, but the soul will awaken us in its own perfect way before things go too far.

When we choose *anything* over love, we miss the mark.
That doesn't mean we need live like monks; it just means
that we need to be constantly aware of the sensibilities
that guide our decisions and fill our days. True success is
founded on warm relationships and deep connections
with all living beings; anything else is just smoke and mir-
rors created by the ego to distract us from the main event.
And of course that distraction never works for long. It is
our inherent nature to wake up to Spirit. Everything that
is not real will become apparent as such and fall away.

Here are some questions that might help you to see
clearly how success can cause a crisis in your life and relationship.

Gauging Success

1. Do you consider your success to be defined by
how much money you make?

2. When things get really busy, do you still make sure there is time for your partner? Or if you are not yet involved with a partner, do you make time for friends and family?

3. As you climb the ladder of your particular occupation, are you as considerate of your partner as when you weren't so successful?

4. Do you find that the more successful you are, the less connected you are to your partner or personal relationships?

5. Does the old adage "It's lonely at the top" apply to you?

6. How does your work requirement affect your family life? Your friendships? Your relationship?

7. Where are you most likely to devote your time and attention?

Only you know where you are putting your energy, where your heart is. If you see that your career is putting your relationship in jeopardy, slow down and really think about what is important to you. We are often nudged by the soul to choose a more authentic life, and if we don't devote ourselves to a soulful path, you can bet there is a correction lying just around the corner. It might come in the form of some sort of personal loss, or perhaps as a midlife crisis. Certainly depression would be a fitting state for the mind to settle into when we know in our bones that we are off course. Or, if we haven't conducted ourselves with integrity, we may even sabotage ourselves as we approach success because we feel unworthy of it.

Remember, you have all the answers you'll ever need. You just need to slow down and get quiet. And listen.

chapter seven

Sacred Partnership

*A human being is a part of the whole called by us "the universe,"
a part limited in time and space. He experiences himself, his
thoughts and feelings, as something separate from the rest—a
kind of optical delusion of consciousness. This delusion is a
kind of prison for us, restricting us to our personal desires and
affection for a few persons nearest to us. Our task must be to free
ourselves from this prison by widening the circle of understanding and compassion to embrace all living creatures and the
whole of nature in its beauty.*

—ALBERT EINSTEIN, *QUANTUM QUESTIONS*

This is when things get really exciting.
As we deepen and expand our own personal consciousness, all our relationships will deepen and expand as well.
It doesn't matter whether or not your partner has signed
up for this curriculum of transformation; all that matters
is that *you* are becoming more aware. As you wake up to
the love within you, you will awaken in your partner—
and everyone around you—that very awareness of love.

As we unravel the knots in our development and patterns of behavior, we inevitably draw out of the people

around us very different—more refined—reactions and responses. The more ably we confront the things that scare us, embrace them, and make peace, the less we will project unfinished business onto our relationships. When we own our "stuff" and work to resolve it, our partners will unconsciously be given permission to do the same for themselves.

Much of this change in how we interact will be subtle. But this is indeed how growth happens for the most part: insights, adjustments, and tune-ups are the order of the day until suddenly you will have rounded a corner or reached a summit.

By bringing into harmony the divergent energies within our own psyche, we have become skilled at smoothing out the glitches within our relationships. Having recognized that most of our shortcomings were really old wounds that required tending to, we have come to better understand and forgive our partner's "faults." Instead of judging, we have learned to see the wisdom inherent in the challenges that have confronted us. We have become more aware of how we are interrelated and are less put off by differences. Instead of reacting out of habit, we act in a more considerate manner, and we have learned to surrender to Spirit what is outside our control. In this way, we have begun to integrate our humanness with our divine nature. As we have cultivated intimacy with our significant other, so have we cultivated an intimacy with God. We have stretched ourselves and begun to embrace our spiritual potential.

As we move into more genuine intimacy and connectedness with our partners, we simultaneously notice something wonderful happening in other areas of our life. We begin to sense that something has come alive inside us, as if that little seed of Spirit within has been activated and is growing at an ever-greater velocity. We feel empowered as the divine moves more freely through our thoughts, words, and deeds. We begin to sense ourselves not only as vessels for love to flow through, but also as architects of a better world. We radiate light and inspire it; and in this way, we will have answered our highest calling.

Now we remember that we are all connected in origin, all joined by the same God who breathes life into each of us. We look into each other's eyes and see not only ourselves, but God winking through. When we honor our partners as if they were Spirit incarnate, we feel the unmistakable presence of the One. God becomes known to us as we freely recognize and love the person standing before us. This is our spiritual practice.

We may sometimes experience this awakening as a tingling throughout our whole being; we may get goose bumps on our arms in moments of "I got it!" or feel a warmth spreading throughout our chest. Often we may begin to laugh, and sometimes we cry at the same time. Something deep within tells us that we are on the right track; we are hitting the mark, making good choices. We feel a newness, a freshness, about our energy. And our natural instinct is to keep the energy moving. We want to share this good feeling, do something to transmit and communicate to those around us the tenderness and power we've begun to access.

Throughout this book, you've learned to go within, to clear away old blockages and reconfigure how you do things. Now it's time to push *out* and expand your life's mission. We can go beyond our previous self-serving limitations and use the temple of partnership to extend the reach of heaven on earth. This is the sacred contract of soul mates.

Offerings

Our spiritual path is always unfolding; we are always receiving impulses to go deeper and expand beyond what our current capabilities are. The message of love is constantly making its way through us, pushing us past our ego needs and distorted perceptions. We are beginning to understand that we are reflections and manifestations of God. We realize that we need not wait around to "find" God or continue to hope that God shines light on our relationship situation, but rather that we can live up to the "God potential" within us. To move to the next stage of Self-realization requires that we enact—or demonstrate—

the powerful love we are coming to know is at our core. The call to grace would have us become more effortful in exerting our power to heal, enliven, and affect the ever-evolving world around us.

Once again love relationships provide an excellent catalyst for moving into and embracing our full potential. Here are three excellent ways of offering your life as an instrument for both intensifying and grounding love: 1. communing with Spirit, 2. creating from your heart, and 3. practicing Partner Tonglen.

Communing with Spirit

If we want to spend more time energized by the clarity and love we have been tapping into, we would do well to establish a ritual of communing with Spirit. It's all too easy to let the surface noise of everyday life break our spiritual momentum. We will always be tempted by our lower nature to blame, judge, or hold each other at bay. We are human, and although we may have elevated ourselves into a higher expression, we still have within us the lower—or denser—aspect of mind. Our old instincts and desires don't simply vanish from our consciousness, but rather they fade into the background and become less and less pronounced. So it's not enough to just intellectually grasp this stuff; we must act on the information regularly to keep the old ways from crowding back in.

I have two Chihuahuas that are not the best-behaved dogs in the world. They regularly bark, nip at people's heels, and mark up the house with their "accidents." I became so exasperated trying to keep them behaving properly that I finally called in a dog trainer, who gave me all sorts of good advice and tricks to use so that the dogs would learn who was master (me, not them!). Much to my relief, they started to act like dogs I could be proud of. The regular exercises the trainer taught me to use seemed to instill order and discipline in their world. And they seemed more secure, less burdened with the responsibility to "hold down the fort" (they stopped going after the FedEx guy and tormenting the neighbors' kids at the fence). They seemed to visibly relax into a more deferential role. I gave myself a little pat on the back and thanked the trainer for helping me work things out.

After things had been going well for a few days, I eased up on the rules. Then I became too busy to do our ten-minute trainings every day. I stopped reaching for the soda can filled with pennies every time they started barking, because it never seemed conveniently at hand. I stopped telling them to sit before I put their food down. I stopped walking them at my pace to show them who was boss and instead let them pull me around at their leisure. And soon enough I forgot altogether what those tricks were that had kept my little monsters in line.

My point in telling this is to illustrate how our less refined tendencies are a lot like untrained little beasts; they will get out of hand as long as there is no one directing them. Our higher mind is like the trainer; it directs us to go about things in the most masterful way. But if we stop our practice as soon as things get good, we'll begin slipping back into the old patterns of acting out.

If we want to become masterful in our lives, and specifically in our relationships, we must remain attentive to our "training." One of the best ways I have found to keep myself focused is to set aside regular time for communing with Spirit. Through prayer and meditation we stay on track, recognizing the "demons" as they come up and then dealing with them lovingly and firmly. We can listen for the still small voice within to inspire us and make us better people and better partners. We can relax into the comfort of knowing that we are pushing ourselves to do our best and leave the rest to God.

It is said that if prayer is asking, then meditation is listening. And just as in a conversation we take turns speaking and listening, so it is with Spirit. It's like a wheel of energy that we keep in motion. By committing to seek out and listen for the message of Spirit for a few minutes each day, our practice will deepen.

Sometimes it's not until we hear ourselves put our feelings into words that we actually know what is going on in our heart of hearts. When I pray, I follow an established sequence. First, I give thanks for all that is good in my life.

Then I ask for forgiveness where I missed the mark, and along with that, the ability to do things differently next time. And lastly, I do my "surrenders," turning whatever issues, problems, or questions I have over to Spirit. Here's an example.

Sample Daily Prayer

Thank you, God, for all that is joyful in my life. For this beautiful view from my veranda, for my health that enables me to enjoy a daily hike, and for my friends who enrich my life with their depth and humor. Thank you for the way my husband believes in me, for the way he thinks I'm interesting and smart no matter what we are talking about. Thank you for the comfort we live in and all the adventurous things we do together. Thank you especially for guiding me to a man who is so caring, intelligent, and fun to be with. I am also grateful, God, for all the opportunities to grow that you have sent my way.

For instance, I can clearly see that I wasn't there for my husband yesterday when he needed me. He was trying to tell me something that was important to him and I shrugged it off because I didn't want to deal with it. I think I was afraid of what he might say; that I might somehow have to change my own behavior. Please forgive me for not rising to my full potential in that moment. And through your forgiveness, please assist me in becoming more kind, more available, and more compassionate. May my ways be amended and may his heart be healed.

And finally, dear God, please take my marriage and let it be of service to you. Help me to let go of all fears and anxieties; help me to know that I am exactly where I am supposed to be. I surrender to you all my preconceptions of what marriage could or should be, and I ask that it reflect an even greater love than I have ever imagined. Let our partnership be deeply enjoyed by both of us, but let it also be used for something bigger than just our happiness. Let all who come within our sphere be lifted by our commitment to and love for each other. May we serve you individually and as a couple in whatever form would best manifest your grace. I surrender to you all the details, and I thank you for leading us into our highest purpose together. Amen.

You can see how the prayer follows the pattern: thanks, confession, surrender. In this way we can be sure to cover all the ground. Because the ego likes to distract us from what is uncomfortable, it is wise to pointedly look for things that need attention. By regularly talking to Spirit *out loud*, we can expose any self-deception or flaws in our behavior. It is a way of keeping ourselves honest and vulnerable. By ritualizing the time, place, and method of prayer, we can be sure to stay alert and attuned to all our inner workings. Perhaps a walk around the block every morning at 7:00 AM would be the perfect ritual for prayer, or sitting in front of an altar for five minutes after the kids have left for school. Even a daily stop into a church or temple can set the perfect tone for regular communion.

When we appeal to God, we are answered. This is not to say that the doors will be flung open immediately and the way will be made instantly clear. But we can rest assured that our relationship is being used in the service of love. As we deepen our partnership with Spirit, it is only natural that our other partnerships will deepen. As we ask for clarity and guidance, we will get the sense that everything is working out perfectly in its own time and way.

Aside from keeping ourselves on track by ritualistically sharing our thoughts with God, prayer is also an excellent way of dealing with conflict, worry, or fear. If something happens and we don't know how to deal with it, we can pray for clarity and strength. We can ask that the highest and holiest thing happen to lift everyone involved in the situation. Prayer is a way of moving energy in the world. We can think on what is wrong and ask that it be changed. By doing this we activate a corrective and counterbalancing energy, which shifts things in both mystical and practical ways. Through prayer, we lend our personal energy and free will to support the unfolding of a more evolved universe. We are not snapping our fingers and insisting on any particular way for something to come about, only that love become evident in the area of our focus. We can say, for example, *"Dear God, my wife and I are so disturbed by the injustices we are reading about in the newspapers these days; please help us to understand what we can do about it. We ask that you bring light to the mind of anybody who might be part of the problem, that they may have an awakening. And since we are all One, God, wherever there is an instinct within us to be unjust, please correct it and replace it with love. Please use us in whatever way we can be of service. May we all be brought around to peace. Amen."* Instead of sitting around and talking about what is wrong, we can join together and ask that love be brought into the picture.

By praying, we are dwelling on a solution, focusing on the transcendent potential in any situation. When it is done correctly, we are not pushing for a particular outcome; instead we are focusing only on bringing divine nature into whatever concerns us. So what if we are unhappy about something our partner is doing and we would like to see it change? Say, for instance, I am deeply concerned over the ethical treatment of animals but my husband does not care about how a cow had to suffer in a factory farm slaughterhouse in order for him to have his steak dinner. Rather than praying for him to become a vegetarian and do things "my way," I could pray that his heart opens to animals and that healing be brought to everyone and everything concerned. My prayer might sound something like, *"Dear God, I thank you for the bond my husband and I share. We are very close in most ways, but I am having difficulty accepting that he does not share my views about consuming meat. I know that you are omniscient and all powerful and so I put this into your hands. In the meantime, please use my energy and my will in the service of making a kinder world for animals. Direct me in all ways of being; tell me what to say and allow me to be of service in every way I possibly can be. Please bless the animals who are suffering every day and let them know peace. Amen."*

By praying about it rather than fighting or making a big issue of our differences, I have directed my energy towards healing and peace without *enforcing* my will on my husband. I can certainly state my case and make it known that this is important to me, but ultimately I have to put into God's hands what I have no control over and ask that the highest thing come about. Prayer is not an act of overcoming someone else's will; it is instead an instrument for subtly transfusing the energy of love into an area of darkness.

Sometimes it's better to say nothing, to have nothing in particular for a goal; sometimes we should just *be*. Where prayer is about activating energy, meditation is about simply being present to the moment and accepting whatever is. In this way Spirit can fill us with inspiration. Instead of worrying, we can just surrender. We can launch the intention to heal and grow, and then gently shrug off the ego's anxieties as they arise.

In physical terms, meditation calms the central nervous system, which, when bombarded by stress, is responsible for anxiety, panic, and depression. Sometimes we don't even know how tightly wound we are until we sit quietly and close our eyes. Then we can breathe deeply and follow our breath; we can pay attention as it comes in and goes out, and thus gently release the tension in our mind and body while at the same time nourishing our sense of well-being and self-esteem.

Because we are all connected to each other, our calm creates calm around us; our willingness to let go allows those around us to stop clinging or holding on to their willfulness. By taking the time to meditate, you are teaching your mind that it can relax and just be, without the chatter supplied by ego. Such a mind is receptive to grace and open to flashes of brilliance.

Many years ago, I had a particularly wonderful flash of brilliance. I was quite frantic at the time. A deadline for some writing was fast approaching. I had a very sick friend in the hospital who needed my constant attention and care. I had errands to run, and I was way behind on my paperwork, which had been piling up on my desk. But I sat down, like I usually do, for at least ten minutes of silent meditation. My mind was racing at first, cluttered with all the thoughts clamoring for my attention, but finally I was able to relax and focus on my breathing. I drifted into the rhythm of the inhale and exhale until suddenly an image of someone I had casually dated popped into my mind. The visual was vivid and I wondered why I couldn't seem to shake it.

After a few more minutes, I concluded my practice and opened my eyes. I thought about this man and began to wonder how he was doing. Our relationship had never taken root because I lived in Los Angeles and he was busy with a career in New York. Also, both of us were still winding down other relationships, so things just didn't seem right at the time.

I thought about our few dates and how much fun he was. The image of his sparkling blue eyes and hearty laugh brought a smile to my face, and I realized that I missed hearing his perspective and listening to his stories. I also remembered how nice it was when he kissed me good night. So I called him and we have been together ever since.

Had I not allowed myself to sit down that day to clear my mind and be in the moment, I might have reunited with the man who was to become my husband anyway, but who knows how many more twists and turns our paths might have taken beforehand. In the total receptivity of my silent mind, his image came to me; thankfully I was able to pay heed.

By slowing down, we become intimate with our authentic Self, the one that knows all the answers and feels untold bliss. By being quiet, the One becomes known to us. The simplest meditation is to sit with your eyes closed and breathe with total attention. You can repeat a mantra, such as *om*, to attune your mind to Spirit, or count your inhales and exhales to focus; but all that is really required is that you sit down and get quiet. Do this once or twice a day for twenty minutes if possible. If that much time seems out of the question, just sit for ten full breaths. After that becomes comfortable, move on to five minutes and then ten. Eventually, twenty minutes will feel natural and enjoyable. You can deepen the effect of your meditation by being *present* as much as you can throughout the day. Don't worry if concerns about the days events push into your mind; just watch them come and go and return your focus to stillness.

When you pray and meditate with your partner, you create a *fellowship of spiritual intent*. You are gathering and harnessing your energies to make a fuller whole. Just like a shared intention, your prayer or meditation gathers momentum and becomes more substantial; it carries more weight and moves with greater power out into the world. Matthew 18:20 says, "Where two or three are gathered together in my name, there am I in the midst of them." This doesn't mean that a church or community group is necessary for being with God; rather, it means that by coming together in the spirit of love, we *affirm God consciousness*. By joining our minds in prayer or meditation, we cultivate a stronger, more unified force field of Spirit.

When we come together in God's name, we call into being the spiritual principles of good will, interconnectedness, and peace. When we join together with our partner for the purpose of spiritual communion, we imbue everyday life with the intention of becoming more spiritually conscious.

Creating From Your Heart

We are all artists, expressing ourselves in different ways. Some of us journal, some of us paint, and some of us sing in the shower. We might be brilliant when it comes to connecting with animals or inspired at creating a garden. But whatever our gift, it is most definitely born of Spirit. You can feel when you click into that sacred energy: your hands move as if by their own volition; ideas flow into your mind as if bubbling up from an endless spring; and everything just melts away as you get lost in that heartfelt celebration. This is nothing less than Spirit at play.

In the Talmud, it says, "You will be called upon to

account for joys not taken." This means it is our *respon-sibility* to be joyful and creative. We don't get a silver star at the end of life because we worked ourselves to exhaustion in pursuit of profit or accomplishment. Life is meant to be explored, and our talents are meant to enrich our realization that Spirit moves through us.

When we unleash our creativity, the mystical within us is made manifest. The whispers of Spirit take form and give us a glimpse of what lies beyond the veil. Our talent is how we communicate from our soul; it speaks of our deepest inner truth. The more we use our gifts, the more we share who we are, and thus the more intimate we become with each other.

I once had a client named Rochelle who came to me because her marriage had become stagnant. Rochelle and Harry had been married for six years and she was beginning to think they wouldn't make it past the seven-year itch. It wasn't that Harry did anything wrong; he was kind and loving, consistently brought in a salary that made their life comfortable, and "would never have even dreamed of cheating." She had no apparent reason for being unhappy, and yet she was, deeply.

I asked Rochelle how her days were spent. Well, Tuesdays were movie nights, Fridays were date nights, and Sundays were always reserved for tennis. Mornings were usually the same: coffee and newspaper, walking the dogs, and going off to their separate jobs. All well and good. But no magic; nothing new to add spark to their conventional routine.

I asked Rochelle what she was doing to fulfill her creative side. She looked at me for a moment and then launched into a litany of excuses. "I'm too busy to take on an artistic project, and there's not enough room in the house for a studio. I work late as it is, and Harry would be lost without dinner on the table at seven." I then asked Rochelle where she found her "juice" for life and how it made its way into the relationship. Again, there was a pause, followed by, "I read the tabloids and tell Harry what all those crazy Hollywood folks are doing. And I take aerobics three times a week so I look good in my tennis clothes for him. It's always fun to go out with our friends together. But mostly, I guess, Harry is the one I look to for inspiration. And he's not doing a very good job." Bingo! Rochelle was looking outside herself for excitement. And poor Harry just kept coming up short.

I told Rochelle that she needed to find an avenue through which she could stir up the energy inside her. "It's inside all of us," I said, "more than we'll ever know what to do with." I recommended that she and Harry take ballroom dancing classes together. At first Rochelle was hesitant, but then she began to chuckle at the idea of dressing up and stepping out with her husband.

After only a month of classes, something shifted in

both Rochelle and Harry. They found themselves immensely enjoying their newfound artistic expression. They began to look at each other in a new and exciting way, almost as if they were beginning their courtship all over again. Since Harry's job didn't allow for much time to take classes, he keenly looked forward to their weekly evening on the dance floor. But Rochelle spent many hours making dance costumes, finding the right music, and signing up for contests. She didn't quit her job or join a dance troupe, but she did indulge her newfound artistic spirit with great enthusiasm.

Needless to say, Rochelle and Harry made it through the seven-year itch, and they're more deeply connected than ever before. Rochelle felt alive and fulfilled and no longer depended on Harry to light her up. When they danced together, she would catch his eye and know that she had found her soul mate after all. Not a soul mate that came perfectly packaged with all the bells and whistles, but a soul mate with whom she committed to sharing her own excitement.

When we give to ourselves, we give to our partners. When we give to our partners, we give to ourselves. And when we can share creativity as a way of celebrating the Spirit within us, we can offer up to each other—and all of those around us—a more tangible experience of God.

Practicing Partner Tonglen

Compassion is a quality that develops naturally as the heart opens; you certainly can't force it, but you *can* shut down to it by just turning a blind eye. I think a lot of cruelty and misery endures in this world because we don't know what to do about it; we think we are powerless to make a difference and so we keep our eyes closed and hope things will get better on their own. But we aren't powerless at all; in fact, as soon as we are willing to be completely awake to what another is experiencing, we can make a big difference in their sense of well being. Remember, Spirit can move readily more through us if we are open, alert, and willing; so if we remain shut down to someone's suffering, we render ourselves helpless to alleviate it. We are all each other's healers. We have to invite in the pain and connect it to where *we* have experienced pain. In this way, we develop empathy and compassion. As we become more in touch and connected with each other, we can really make a difference—both in our relationship and in the world.

Let's look at this in terms of your relationship. If your partner is suffering somehow—emotionally, physically, or spiritually—you might try various ways of cheering them up, but at a certain point you would likely realize that none of your efforts make much of a difference.

If you want to be masterful in your relationship, ask

yourself what a spiritual master would do in this situation. A master would not run from another's suffering;
they would not just *talk* about having compassion. They
would be fiercely present in the face of the pain and actually be willing to take the suffering into their own heart.
This is not martyrdom, or even co-dependence, but
rather a calling up of the inborn capacity to relate and
heal. If we want to attain enlightenment, we must overcome our ego (self-centered fear) and help others along
their way by sharing their burden. That spirit of service
is crucial in moving humanity forward.

The following is a method of offering relief to someone
who is impaired, wounded, or struggling in some way.
Tonglen is an ancient—and up until recently, secret—
Tibetan Buddhist meditative practice that actually means
"taking and sending." It was initially performed at the
bedside of someone who was dying to ease their suffering.
The Tonglen practitioner would breathe in the dying person's pain and send them back peace. By doing so, one is
saying, "I will witness and take in your suffering so you do
not have to bear it alone. Use my strength and light to help
you through this." It is a generous and courageous practice, and it engenders mastery over our own fears.

Tonglen is useful in relationships when you want to assist your partner in moving through something, but the
practice is also useful when *your* "stuff" comes up around
them. When they do something that would normally up-

set you, instead of judging or acting out against it, you can breathe it in and befriend it. You can soften to the struggle and make peace by your willingness to change out your partner's pain energy for the tenderness you are accessing within yourself.

I have respectfully modified the practice so that it fits into the context of spiritual growth through the vessel of relationship. Here's how to do it: close your eyes and get very quiet, centering yourself. Sense that God is within and all around you, and know that you are being held in this, the most healing and miraculous light. Then imagine your partner in your mind's eye; notice where they are hurting or require some sort of healing. As you breathe in, breathe in their pain. See it as thick, dark, and full of every unpleasantness. Take it all down into your heart, knowing that at your center is God's heart, and hold it there for a moment. Then, when you exhale, send back pure, clean energy from that radiant Source within you. See the new energy as clear and luminous. Picture your partner receiving joy and peace, being completely set free from suffering. Continue inhaling and exhaling like this until you sense there is no more negativity in them; see them completely absolved of anything that might disturb them.

Then move beyond your partner to his or her family, doing the same thing—inviting their suffering into your heart and then sending back purified, enlightened energy until you sense they are freed from all their pain. Extend the cleansing breath into the past and let it radiate out into the future. Take your time. See generations being healed, ancestral lines of souls released from all that ails them. And then, as you continue breathing, expand your practice to include the suffering of all sentient beings in the town or city where you live; then your country. Finally, extend your generosity to the entire world. Breathe in all that is foul or harmful; hold it while it is transmuted by Spirit; and then send it back as purity, joy, light, and freedom. Feel a sense of expansion, of non-resistance. Do this until you feel there is no more work to do, nothing left to take in for the time being. Then just gently get in touch with your own breath and notice the compassion swelling in your heart for your partner and for all mankind. Most of all, feel the enormous joy of knowing you have moved energy in a masterful way. When you feel ready, open your eyes.

There is no timetable for this practice; it is entirely up to you. You might start off with five minutes and increase the meditation over time to as many as thirty or sixty minutes, if that feels right. Really, time has nothing to do with it; the real issue is how deeply you can connect to your compassion and how intently you can focus on your vision of healing. Practicing Partner Tonglen teaches you not to avoid pain, but rather to be with it. When you are present to something, it no longer can grab hold of you because there is nothing in you—no fear or avoidance—to hook into. This non-resistance makes you more fully alive because you are no longer safeguarding or putting walls around your heart. You are letting in the truth of what is, thus making yourself a deeper and more compassionate person. By doing this, all your relationships—romantic and otherwise—will become deeper and more connected. When we soften to someone's darkness, we soften to ourselves. We become less ego oriented and more in touch with our divine nature.

My friend Karen is married to a wonderful painter, Sam, who works in the detached garage outside their house. Being an artist, Sam tends to be very sensitive. Unfortunately, sometimes his moods sink into a downward spiral and he goes into long periods of depression. Karen tried all sorts of things to cheer him up; she appealed to him with logic, reminding him of the good reviews critics gave his work and the steady sales that proved he was striking a chord with people. She tried getting him to stop drinking alcohol and eating sugar, hoping that maybe his chemistry would right itself given the proper diet. She tried planning trips to the beach or hikes in the mountains, thinking that the fresh air would snap him out of it. But Sam remained depressed and withdrawn despite her best efforts.

When I told Karen about Partner Tonglen, she resisted. "Why would I want to take all his gunk into myself?" she asked. "Won't I then be absorbing his negative energy?" I explained to her that it wasn't Karen who would be taking it in, but Spirit, which would be working *through* her.

I reminded her that this practice was about tapping into her compassion rather than trying to willfully fix or change anything. Partner Tonglen was a way that she could help Sam without intruding.

When Karen first breathed in Sam's sadness, she felt scared; it was so heavy, she said, and complicated with all sorts of memories and projections. I coached her not to focus on details, but to *feel* the energy rather than intellectualize it. As she did this, she said she began to sense that she was melting into some great force that had always been just beneath the surface of her personality. Her desperation at not being able to make a difference for Sam gently began to lift, and she felt a quiet confidence as she continued to send him love and peace.

For the next few days she did Partner Tonglen for five minutes at a time, and Sam remained in his depression. But for Karen, he seemed less "dug in to" his sadness; it was as though she had stopped feeding it with her resistance. Even though her intention with Tonglen was to help Sam, Karen was actually feeling lighter herself. She stopped outwardly focusing on making Sam better and got on with the business of her own days.

When Sam "came out the other side" of his brooding, Karen felt happy for him, but she didn't feel responsible in any way. She knew he was in the hands of God, and that—in her words—she had helped deliver him there. Now whenever anything comes up, whether it is a fight or impending depression, Karen practices Partner Tonglen. Sam never knew the specifics of what she was doing in her meditation, but he recently confided that he felt an intense closeness to her that he had never experienced before. Karen told him, with a smile to herself, that she too was feeling very intimate with him.

By practicing Partner Tonglen, we not only give service to the person on whom we are focusing, but we also practice pushing past all our old ego needs. We're not trying to be *right*, not trying to change them or show them where they have taken a wrong turn. Instead we are there for them in the quiet hands-off space of meditation. We aren't trying to *control* or dictate our partner's path; we only send loving energy to support them in being happy and released. We aren't endeavoring to *distract* ourselves from pain but rather are choosing to stay present to the truth of what is. We aren't trying to *feel superior or inferior*, because we are exchanging their energy for our own and thus coming to better understand ourselves as equal and interchangeable. By "taking and sending," we learn to relax the boundaries between self and other, and so move more deeply into the experience of Oneness. We are reminded that we are all interconnected, that if one of us suffers, all of us suffer, and if one of us can find peace, all of us can. By practicing this meditation of compassion, we become more masterful in spreading loving-kindness throughout the world, starting right at home with our partners.

Folding in the Lessons and Gifts

As we look back over the history of our relationships, we can see that we were drawn to each other for very specific reasons. The lessons we needed to learn unfolded exactly as they should have. Our partners have been our companions, our lovers, and our guides, and we have been theirs. Through the avenue of soul mate love, both partners have evolved into more integral and empowered people. It is as if there has always been a divine design bringing about exactly what we needed in order to move into higher consciousness. Of course some of the lessons have been difficult ones, but knowing what we do, we would likely not choose to change a thing.

Through the lens of partnership, we have come to know ourselves more intimately. We have witnessed our intense reactions to things our partners have said or done and allowed them to point out what needed to be attended to or healed in our own psyches. We've learned to stay present to the tempest of emotions that naturally rises and falls in the course of daily life. We've released some old behaviors and tested new and more high-minded ones.

We have come to realize how our own spiritual development is wholly tied up with our ability to create an intimate union with another. As we see the grace and perfection in our partner, we are better able to experience those qualities in all of life. Such is the promise of soul mate love.

As we become ever more conscious, so does our relationship. By attuning to Spirit within us, we become aware of Spirit all around. We have set in motion a vigorous and authentic journey of transformation; we are firmly on the path of enduring soul mate love. As we shift our attention from getting what we want to understanding life's deeper mysteries, we can begin to see the grand design being played out in the fields of romance.

At this point, it might be illuminating to look back on every significant love relationship you've been party to. As you see the value in each experience, you will recognize the all-knowing power of Spirit. Let's look at what you learned from those past liaisons that led you to this point in time.

The History of Love at Work in Your Life

Make a list of each person you have ever been romantically involved with, leaving enough space after the name to write extensively.

1. Under each name, write about what originally attracted you to them.
2. Try and recall conflicts that arose and how you dealt with them.
3. Consider how those conflicts were useful to your growth. How did your soul expand through that experience?

4. Is there anything outstanding that needs to be addressed, forgiven, or amended? If so, how can you take care of that?

5. Do you recognize the holy contract each of you had with the other?

6. How does the relationship that ended still live in you and contribute to your relationship with the One?

7. In the silence of your heart, wish that person knowledge of your love and see only peace between you.

By taking stock of the gifts we received through past relationships, we can better appreciate and trust the mystery that moves throughout our partnership now. No matter how difficult or mundane or exciting things get, Spirit is always in motion, bringing us into a richer and more loving Self.

In reviewing the past, what becomes obvious is where there were opportunities to heal, and where we had the chance to be kind and humane; those opportunities repeated themselves many times in different ways, and sometimes we took them and sometimes we didn't. Those occasions when we transcended our lower instincts were victories of the soul. Through them, we became ever more intimate with the ways of God. Let those triumphs inspire you to reach for more.

We can choose how quickly and how well we integrate our lessons and accept our gifts. We can "get it" in an instant, or we can open ourselves painstakingly and only under duress. The heartbreaking moments are the ones where you *know* you didn't get it right. You could have acted differently but fell into an old, self-serving or Self-sabotaging pattern. Looking back you can see that the same challenge was waiting right around the corner to give you, once again, a chance to be masterful.

As you take stock and see where you didn't quite rise to the occasion, instead of beating yourself up or feeling ashamed of how you acted, just notice it. See what you can learn from your review. And then surrender; actively surrender your behavior to Spirit, asking that you be brought back into alignment with its all-pervasive wisdom.

Now that we've reviewed how love played a role in your past, let's take a look at your current situation.

Enlightenment at Work in Your Present Partnership

1. What was it that initially drew you to your partner or present person of interest?
2. What were the things you needed to learn and how was that made possible?
3. How have you been changed by knowing them?

4. What are the gifts of his or her soul that you
   have not accepted?

5. Which of your gifts have you withheld?

6. Do you recognize that you still have opportunities to grow?

7. What can you do in the context of this relationship to more fully embrace the love that is
   within and all around you?

The answers to these questions are what make up the
stuff of life. We are learning to love, learning to widen the
circle of connectedness in the world. At the moment of
death, when our lives flash before our eyes, we will not
see the details of who did what to whom. We will only see
how love made us vulnerable and how we responded. All
the rest will fade to black, and we will know it for the illusion that it was.

When we look at the big picture, we can see how the
curriculum of relationships serves us; we can see how
grace continues to make itself known through the ups and
downs of partnership. And this is what soul mate love requires of us: that we keep engaging in the questions that
will draw us ever closer to the infinite connection with
Spirit.

Whenever we can shift the tide from fear to love, we
become more enlightened partners. It may come in the

quietest of moments or it may take the form of a grand epiphany, but each step takes us deeper into the love we had always hoped was waiting for us. It is in the warm embrace, the wink of an eye, or the nod of recognition to the person who stands before us that we come to know the One, *the creator who is not separate from the created.*

That person who at first we regarded as partner we now see has been the Teacher all along. By reaching for soul mate love, we have learned to transcend our limitations. We have ascended to new levels of relating, new ways of being. We are building bridges and closing gaps; we are becoming the connective fibers in a glorious web of love. We are responding to the sacred charge of bringing salvation not only to each other, but to the whole world.

There is nothing more to search for, nothing more to try and attain. We are here with the Beloved. Look in the mirror. Look into your partner's eyes. Look deeply until you see God looking back at you and so it is that you will know the One.

May you know the love that is within and all around you. May you let that love be expressed and known to all those who come in contact with you. May you be blessed by the One and may you bless the world with the gift of your Self.

Acknowledgments

I am so grateful for all the assistance and kind support that has ushered me along my way in writing this book. It really does take a village.

To the folks at William Morris: Jennifer Rudolph Walsh, my agent, who, from the very beginning, saw the potential and worked relentlessly to get the manuscript in shape and to the right people; Jim Wiatt who has steadfastly assured me that I am on course; and Eric Zohn whose advice and introduction led me to the right professional home.

To the brilliant and creative team at Miramax Books: Harvey Weinstein who has the magic touch with any and all creative projects; Rob Weisbach, Judy Hottensen, Kristin Powers, Katie Finch and JillEllyn Riley, all of whom I am humbled and privileged to work with. To Jonathan Burnham who opened the door and welcomed me in, I am greatly honored. Also, thank you to Ellen Rosenblatt for her typesetting. To Melanie Dunea for capturing the light in such a lovely way. And a big thanks to Peter Guzzardi, my editor, for expertly riding herd over my words.

To Debi Dion, Nancy DiToro, Kevin Law, and Olivia Rosewood for their inspired help and contributions.

And, of course, to my husband Tom, without whom I would not have learned what I know thus far. He is my partner, my love, my soul mate.

Please visit my website www.kathyfreston.com for more information or to order guided meditation CDs.